THE LAST BOY IN AUSCHWITZ

MOSHE (MJETEK) BOMBERG

ReadMore Press

DISCOVERING THE NEXT BESTSELLER

Sign up for Readmore Press' monthly newsletter and get a
FREE audiobook!

For instant access, scan the QR code

Where you will be able to register and receive
your sign-up gift, a free audiobook of

Beneath the Winds of War
by **Pola Wawer,**

which you can listen to right away

Our newsletter will let you know about
new releases of our World War II historical
fiction books, as well as discount deals and
exclusive freebies for subscribed members.

"And God said to Satan:
Behold, he is in your hands; but spare his life."

Job 2:6

Anything But His Soul
Moshe (Mjetek) Bomberg

With the assistance of the Memorial Foundation
for Jewish Culture, New York

First Edition: 1976
Translation from The Hebrew: Zoe Jordan

Contact: yoavbomberg@gmail.com
ISBN 9798865831440

THE LAST BOY IN AUSCHWITZ

A WW2 Jewish Holocaust Survival True Story

MOSHE (MJETEK) BOMBERG

I.

An Incident between Warsaw and Ostrowiec

I was sitting on the 7 pm train from Warsaw. In my pocket was a ticket that was to deliver me to the town of Ostrowiec Świętokrzyski in the early morning to "visit" my aunt, my mother's sister who had lived in that small city for many years.

The rickety train shook and swayed forcefully. The wheels rattled and screeched but inside the car, quiet prevailed. I sat beside the window looking out, though there was nothing to see—the darkness was heavy. I looked at the glass window. The dim light inside the car and the darkness outside made a mirror of the windowpane, in which the other side of the car was clearly reflected. I noticed again, perhaps for the twentieth time, the strange look of the passenger sitting on the bench in the corner. I did not move. I was paralyzed by fear that clouded my thinking.

We set off from Warsaw, and from the ghetto. The year—1940, in which the Jews were imprisoned in a ghetto beyond a wall that rose four meters or more, the top of which twinkled with broken glass. I knew the wall well—I had lived in the ghetto for a long time. I used to look at it in the evenings on our way back from work, despite my terrible exhaustion. The train was a regular Polish train, but with a German conductor—a swastika on his uniform and the zeal of Hitler shining from his eyes. And me—

Jewish, naive, fleeing, nobody. I was 17 years old, a former slave laborer for the Germans until just four hours ago, after much preparation, fear, and doubt.

My father, mother, my brother Yehezkel, and I left to save ourselves from the Warsaw ghetto. We ripped the identifying blue armbands with the stars of David off of our sleeves, concealed ourselves in a hiding place in the factory where we worked and waited until the appointed time when we were to emerge and set out for the train station. We took special care with Mother. She was going to have to leave the ghetto in plain sight, during the shift of the Polish policeman who now possessed the last of our most valuable treasures: Mother's jewelry and the heavy silver candlesticks that we had taken great pains to hide until now. Mother was going to have to walk quickly and confidently to the train station, linger for some time in the public restroom, and wait for us beside the old newspaper stand. Would she manage it? Would we all manage?

We managed. At nearly seven in the evening, the train's departure time, I approached the ticket office. All around were Polish policemen, Nazi policemen, and amateur "police"—Poles who roamed and kept a close watch for "finds" to denounce. Although I was the youngest of all of us, I had the "best" face—a typical Polish face that would not arouse suspicion, and an accent to match. As such, I was designated as the family representative for "public relations."

At the ticket office I requested four tickets to Ostrowiec and casually placed the money in front of the clerk. He didn't so much as glance up at me. Without speaking, my father boarded the second to last train car, I boarded the fourth, and my mother and brother got on together, her leaning on his arm, the poignant sight of a mother supported on the arm of her son dressed in work clothes. We separated so that if one of us was caught, the rest of the family would remain undiscovered.

My sister Miriam had already been at our aunt's place for a few months. She had gone there before the Germans invaded Poland. We informed her to stay put and not to return to Warsaw. The small and distant city of Ostrowiec was much safer than Warsaw. Even now, while in the Warsaw ghetto, many people were dying of hunger every day, and the Jews of Ostrowiec were in their homes, eating more or less their fill.

Again, I glanced over at the windowpane. The man in the corner was still staring at me. I sat silently for a while, feeling that I could not stand the awful tension. I slowly rose, stretched my arms a little, as though I had just gotten up to get some air, and stepped outside. I stood on the small platform that connected the two train cars. The platform's floor moved back and forth. It had no roof, and only two iron chains, one on either side. I held on to a chain with my back turned to the door of the train car I had just exited.

When I felt a heavy hand on my shoulder, I did not jump as I had thought I would. I slowly turned my head and said in my regular voice, in fluent Polish, "What can I do for you?"

My fear was coming true. It was the same passenger that had been watching me all that time. He shrugged and asked sharply, "Where are you from?"

Not politely, deferential, as was customary, rather, "you," as if I were his friend or as if he knew exactly who I was, the Jew. I did not take offense. A Jew fleeing on a Polish train run by Nazis cannot permit himself to take offense.

"I am from Warsaw," I answered.

"Are you running away from Warsaw or what?" To the point,

not mincing words...

"What are you talking about?"

"We know you!" He erupted, and to keep his balance, he grabbed a link of the chain connecting the car. "You suck our blood!"

"Excuse me, sir!" I replied, suitably angry.

I did not feel much agitation. It was as if I was standing and observing other people conversing. But he, his face shining in the dim light that came through the tiny window, continued, "Just wait, when we get to the station, you'll see, I'll fix you, Jew!"

I did not answer. I fully believed him.

That same moment, the car door opened again, and a man came out. He was about forty or forty-five, dressed in a shabby old suit. As I watched him closely, he turned to me and said clearly, "What happened, Teddek? Why did you go out?"

My name was not Teddek. I was called Mjetek. I had never seen him before in my life. I was no less astonished by him than by the anti-Semitic Pole standing beside me.

"What does he want from you, this criminal?" he asked, eying the informer with a deadly stare.

The informer snapped out of it before I did, "This is a Jew I tell you! A Jew! He's running away from the ghetto! You don't even know him! You weren't sitting together in there! He must be taken care of!"

It was a strange scene, the three of us, squashed together on that narrow platform, swaying under our feet and shaking audibly, and the heavy darkness closing in all around.

"Are you crazy?" demanded the man in the shabby suit, looking him over with deep disgust. "Running away? I know him. He's Polish!"

"What? You're sorry for this Jew? You're a friend of Jews!

Maybe you are also Jewish? We can send you away too! Don't worry, let's just get to the station and we'll see!"

His eyes glimmered with the thought of the reward he would get from the German gendarmerie for handing over a Jew: half a liter of vodka or two kilograms of sugar, his choice. Not a bad price for one Jew. And here he might even have two Jews...

The old Pole was quiet a moment. He pulled a crushed cigarette out of his pocket, put it between his lips, and asked the Nazi: "Got any matches?"

He was taken aback by the turn in the conversation and reached into his pocket to get a box of matches. And here things happened at an incredible speed—at that moment the old man grabbed my shoulder with one hand to steady himself and with the other pushed the informant with all his might into the darkness. We heard him cry out in horror, but the passengers inside could not hear a thing over the rattling of the train. Even if they had heard, it is doubtful that anyone would wish to know what had happened. It was a time in which people were mostly looking out for themselves...

The two of us remained. For a moment there was quiet on the platform. I did not look up nor meet the man's gaze. A Jew in Poland in the year 1940 had no friends. I had been saved by a miracle. He pushed me toward the train car.

"Come," he said, "come, we're going inside!" And in a low voice he added, "Don't worry, I'll look after you. It's alright. The main thing is that you hold it together."

Hold it together until when, I thought. I did not say a word.

We went inside and sat down beside one another. Throughout the journey he spoke to me, and I answered to the best of my ability. We spoke about light matters: cinema, sport, and the challenges of earning a living. We discussed everything except politics and the Germans, and certainly not about the informant that had fallen off the moving train. We were chatting amicably, as if it were normal, all the while listening for a siren or search, but it appeared that the noise of the train had helped us that night. No one suspected what had happened.

The train came to a stop. We had arrived at Ostrowiec Świętokrzyski. I departed as good-naturedly as I was able and quietly added, "Thank you!"

I disembarked into the night and found myself in a different world—a world of quiet, lit by the moon, with the crickets chirping. The war had not yet arrived here. I left the station and joined up with my father, mother, and brother. We walked along the small, quiet streets and knocked on the door of my aunt's house.

My astonished sister fell upon us, with tears of dumbfounded happiness. We sat, talking in the darkness for a long time. Quietly we told of what had been happening in recent months.

II.

The Germans Occupy Warsaw

Warsaw held out against the Germans for three weeks. In those days, the Poles were in the same boat as us. We suffered hunger and thirst; we stood together in lines for a loaf of bread; most of what we ate was potatoes. The bombings did not stop. When a horse was killed one street over and people were seen running with knives in their hands, I did not hesitate—I grabbed a knife from the kitchen and I too took a cut of meat. I rushed home, the meat dripping blood along the road. I did not tell my mother what kind of meat it was and she cooked it without asking. To my great surprise the meat was actually very tasty. We felt full again for a short while.

Warsaw's battle was stubborn and courageous, but short-lived. The trenches and barricades on which the residents of the city had worked together with all their strength, could not withstand the German tanks and aircraft bombings. The battle ended with a speech from the city's mayor on the radio: "We have no choice, Warsaw is in a desperate situation. We have no choice. We are forced to open the gates of Warsaw to the Germans."

The German planes stopped bombing; again masses of people were seen in the streets. After some time, the planes returned and people began to run to shelters, but the fleeing stopped when they saw that instead of bombs they were throwing colorful posters, cheerful and reassuring: "Don't worry. Finally, you will get some good German treatment!" the posters proclaimed in big letters, "The Germans want what is best for you. The Germans will make sure you will not want for a thing..."

The first Germans to enter the city were riding three-wheeled motorcycles, wearing gleaming helmets and serious faces, keeping lines that were straight and precise. Behind them appeared trucks full of soldiers. Crowds of Poles stood in the streets and watched them silently. German speakers announced that bread would be distributed in central plazas to anyone who asked. Masses began to rush towards the city centers where German soldiers threw hundreds of loaves of bread from the trucks. Suddenly a commotion came through the crowd—someone had spotted a small German plane hovering low, and shouting was heard: "Stop taking bread! The Germans are photographing us!" The proud people suffered a sudden attack of shame. Here and there people were inciting the crowd to stop accepting the gifts, but many did not respond to the cry, and rather took their loaves of bread and quickly disappeared into the side streets.

Warsaw quickly returned to its usual bustle. The shops and bakeries that had closed with the German invasion reopened. Shopkeepers were no longer afraid of the robberies in which hooligans broke into shops, mostly during bombings, looting food items, clothing, and appliances. The people ruled the streets again. But the ruins all around and the effect of the Germans in uniform that had surfaced all over Warsaw filled our hearts with fear.

It soon became clear that there were thousands of Poles of German descent in Poland, which constituted, in fact, a kind of fifth enlistment. As soon as the Germans occupied, they joined them openly and would appear in the streets, proudly wearing the swastika and carrying themselves with importance. They were appointed to positions and were at the right hand of the German occupiers. They knew everything and reported everything, prepared lists and provided essential information. It became evident that they had been organized and ready well before the occupation, intently awaiting the arrival of the Germans.

We, the Jews, were worried, but not too seriously. We still were not that different from the Polish people around us, we still did not feel the "preference" of the Germans toward the Jews. Soon enough we would fully feel the special treatment directed at us.

The third month after the Germans entered Warsaw was when the propaganda against the Jews began. They did not announce their intentions but began to prime the Polish people and slowly and cautiously sow the seeds of hatred.

Hatred towards the Jews was not new in Poland. Already, in 1938, with the rise of Polish militarism, antisemitism was growing stronger. It was known that here and there, windows of Jewish shops were smashed and Polish gangs would beat up Jews. Hateful signs ridiculing us appeared in the streets, claiming that "the Jew is a cheater and a thief, do not do business with him," and the like. Many Jews were afraid to go out into the streets after dark, and you would not find a Jew in the late show at the cinema. But all of this was within the scope of general unpleasantness, not actual danger.

The Germans turned the matter into an explicit and wide-reaching problem. They needed the cooperation of the peoples among whom we lived, and with German precision, they set the stage for their deeds. The first stage of the German hate propaganda was the caricatures, most of which were copied from Goebbels' newspaper, *Der Sturmer*. Fences, shops, notice boards, everything was covered with the "notorious" Jewish faces—distorted faces with hooked noses. There were cheap jabs at Jewish stereotypes and their control of key roles, and the fact that they held positions that "you, the Pole, could have if they knew their place." Many Poles seemed to read these posts and nod their heads in agreement. The caricatures and the proclamations spoke to the sentiment of the masses. The seeds of hatred sprouted at tremendous speed.

The second stage was the directive that each Jew must wear a white ribbon with a blue Star of David on his left sleeve. A date was set, after which any Jew not wearing such a ribbon would be punished. Jews gathered in their homes and discussed the matter and each, in their way, prepared the ribbons and observed the blue symbol with mixed feelings. The common belief was that this would pass. The Jews were used to suffering, and everything would come to an end sooner or later. But it quickly became clear that the Germans had further plans for the Jews. The community was ordered to submit lists of the names of its members, in order to create jobs for the Jews. From the outset they announced that it would be forced labor—every Jewish man would have to work for the German army two days a week.

The organization of the forced labor was imposed on the community. Comprehensive lists were updated, messages were sent by post to every family, and workplaces and days were assigned. The message would read something like: on such and such days you must present yourself at such and such a place, and so forth. When we reported to the appointed place, we were divided into groups as required: to the airfield, the Gestapo, the different factories, and other places. Meanwhile, many Jewish shops were confiscated and taken over by Poles or Germans. Many Jews were afraid to walk to their shops and simply abandoned them in advance. But not all of the Poles gave in to the Germans plans. There were still proud Poles, discontent with the German occupation.

III.

Underground Activity in Warsaw

In the past, life in our house on Chmielna Street had been pleasant and peaceful. My father made his living as a barber in his own shop beside our house. At first, my brother Yehezkel assisted him, until eventually he opened a barbershop of his own. All of us were members of the youth movement, and I was a devoted member of "Hashomer Hatzair." Our meetings were bursting with enthusiasm—stories of the Promised Land were fascinating and we knew that our ultimate goal was to get to Israel. When the Polish government forbade the continued operation of the various national societies, most disguised themselves as athletic clubs and continued in their activities.

In our group, sport was already an important feature. Each of us devoted himself to the sport he loved most and secretly, unobserved, we also continued our Zionist work. My favorite sport was wrestling, and I excelled at it. When I was fourteen, my brother's friends invited me to watch a wrestling competition held for them at the Workers' Athletic Association (R.K.S. "Skra"). The president of the association was Senator Drovner, a socialist leader in Poland. I participated in competitions, beating many competitors, and was invited to join the association. I accepted, and despite my young age, I was included in the members' various secret activities. I trained nearly every evening and, slowly but surely, I became very agile. My body grew stronger and I grew able to beat competitors much older than myself.

I reached the peak of my victories during the Warsaw wrestling competitions, when I beat many opponents, including a Polish policeman who did particularly well, and won second place, the second-best in Warsaw. But my glory brought bitter fruit: the same policeman bore a most unsportsmanlike grudge against me. As the antisemitism in Warsaw grew stronger, so too did his scrutiny of my family. He made all of our lives miserable with his particular attention to us and made sure that we closely obeyed all orders. When the Germans entered our city, his power over us grew, and many times, I would cry out to my parents that if only I could fight him again, I would "accidentally" break his neck! But I did not get the opportunity to fight him or any other Pole in the ring again. I was no longer an athlete or a competitor. I was in a new category now: "Jew."

Our association went underground. The Germans searched high and low for members of the national societies and imprisoned them one after another. But this did not discourage us. We held secret gatherings disguised as dances, each time hosted by a different member. Some weeks later, a few days before one of the meetings that had been planned in advance, one of the members appeared at our house to let me know that the Germans had gotten ahold of the list of members and had already begun to make arrests. Only later did we learn that this was not the case. Although there were several denunciations, the list had not been found but had been destroyed by the leaders themselves. My friend went on to warn further members, and I grabbed my coat and went straightaway to my uncle's house, far from our place. A few days later my mother came to take me back home.

But that was not the only reason for her trip—notices of forced labor were coming one after another. One man per family was no longer enough. My brother had been outside of Warsaw with the Polish army, retreating from the city at the time of its surrender, and we did not know what had become of him. We were afraid to report this, lest we be "blacklisted." My father could not meet the work demands alone. That same day I went to an afternoon shift in my father's place.

We worked at the airport, repairing flight paths and preparing new ones. The work was not easy, but my young age and strong body held up. One evening, when I returned from work, my father greeted me with a worried expression on his face. Inside, he pointed to a package that had been placed under the bed, tied with a ribbon.

"Someone was here. He said he was from the association. He asked that you hide this and only give it to the person who tells you the password..."

His face showed worry and anger all at once: "But you are just a child! Why must you be put at risk? Your brother is gone, and you are risking too much..."

From the weight and shape of the package, I understood that it contained pamphlets. I knew that many who had been caught in possession of such pamphlets were not seen again but I also knew that I could not refuse. I stuffed the package deep into the laundry closet and covered it with dirty washing. I could not find a better hiding place...

This was repeated several times. After a few days, the package was taken and others replaced it. Along with concern, I felt pride. I realized that I had become a member of the Polish underground. Indeed, after a while, I was called upon for some real action. My friends agreed that my face would not arouse suspicion if they brought me with them, as long as I was not wearing my Jewish armband. We would go out to the street, traveling in a group, enter the cinema and sit noisily in the balcony. In the darkness, we would take the pamphlets out of our pockets, spread them with glue from a tube, and plaster them onto the seats in front of us and behind us, on the armrests and the walls. We would duck out some time before the movie ended, usually in pairs, talking loudly as we left about how boring the film was... Sometimes we added cursing and whistling. Surprisingly, our brazenness actually discouraged the audience. Nobody commented except for an occasional grumble about the disturbance. We appeared to be too confident. When light flooded the theater during the break, the audience saw the notices, calling upon Polish pride, for people to rebel against accepting the Germans. With time, we perfected our methods of distributing the flyers and were always as wary as possible of spies and informers.

For me, this was an exciting adventure, and I did not allow myself to consider the danger. My time was divided between shifts of forced labor and attending the association's meetings and operations.

But the noose around the Jews was tightening. A statement was published in polite and matter-of-fact language to gather any radios and furs possessed by Jews and to bring them to the German police. After several Jews were detained for hiding a radio or fur, then taken for questioning after which they disappeared, a stream of furs and radios went to the Germans. Even then everyone said that this was just a new type of pogrom and that it too would pass...

Most of the youth movements fell apart under the worsening conditions. Schools were closed. The cloud hovering over us was darker than ever, but there were happy days in our home—my brother Yehezkel returned to us. Following the excitement of the reunion, he told us that the far-off military encampment he had been in had surrendered entirely to the Germans. The captured soldiers were sorted and transferred to different camps, and during the transfer he had managed to hide and remain hidden until the camp was evacuated. Afterward, he fled to the fields, buried his Polish uniform in the land of one of the peasants, from whom he bought old civilian clothes for a tidy sum. He told his story drily and concisely, but his eyes betrayed his feelings. We knew that he had had a difficult time, but we refrained from questioning him further.

On the first day back he stayed at home, but the following day he also went to work. He had little time to rest in his room and in his bed—shortly afterward it was announced that a ghetto had been set up for the Jews, who would have to relocate without delay. Father, quick to obey, argued that there was no point in waiting. "With the Germans, there is no room for cleverness," he said. "They will not change their minds!"

We visited the area declared as the ghetto and managed to find a three-bedroom apartment belonging to a Pole on Leszno Street at the corner of Ogrodowa. Since we were among the first to move, the Pole agreed to what seemed to him a tempting offer: to exchange his apartment for our more spacious one, situated in a Polish area. He had no idea that only days later he could have gotten much better offers. With a handcart, we moved only the essentials: clothes, kitchenware, bedding, and the like. Bargaining began between the Jews and their Polish neighbors, who acquired property for pennies—treasures that had been acquired by Jews over generations through manual labor, industriousness, and cleverness. Even shops were sold, sometimes for just a few sacks of flour or potatoes.

Again, we were out of work. The barbershops were sold, cutting off our sources of income. We found new ways to make a living, beginning by trading in work. Work had been assigned to all Jews, rich and poor alike. Among the rich, there were many who did not wish to labor and would pay others to work in their place. Workers' names were not checked, only their numbers. So on our days off, we worked in exchange for pay with which we bought food.

You could still cross to the Polish side and there were trade and business transactions between the ghetto and the city outside of it. But soon the day came when Polish builders began to construct a wall around the ghetto, assisted by the Jewish forced laborers. The wall had a width of about half a meter and rose to a height of four and a half meters. Sharp bottle shards lined the top. Several gates were set up, next to which were stationed Polish and German police. The confinement was complete, with the Jews isolated from the outside world.

The isolation also impacted my activity in the underground; all the while I had made an effort to maintain connection with my fellow members, and they did not forget me, despite the dangerous label assigned to me as a Jew. From time to time, I got news of their actions, and even greetings and requests for information as to what was happening within the ghetto. All that time I went about like a wrestler that had been toppled to the floor of the ring, listening for the count and struggling to get up and return to the fight. My friends outside pressed me to come out and join them; they pointed out my Polish face and asked me to take advantage of my appearance. But I could not go and leave my family in the ghetto. We prepared a plan to get all of us out. The conditions in the ghetto were getting worse; bodies, dead of starvation, were already being seen in the street;

thieves, caught for stealing food, were shot by policemen; and the Jewish Burial Society carts dragged through, gathering up the corpses. Several actions were also carried out, after which the beggars disappeared from the streets for some time. We came to the conclusion that the Germans intended to kill all of the Jews in the ghetto by starvation and disease. We told ourselves that outside, in the small cities, it was less dangerous, and with their proximity to the villages, surely their food supply was better.

We devised a plan to leave for Ostrowiec Świętokrzyski, to my aunt. This was pushed mainly by my mother, whose longing and concern for my sister Miriam was becoming unbearable. We took our valuables out from their hiding place—one of my Polish friends contacted a more enlightened Polish policeman who guarded one of the gates at particular hours. Coordination was crucial to inform us and to organize our departure for work at the appropriate time interval. After protracted discussions, bargaining, and a certain degree of veiled threat, my friends were able to convince the Polish policeman to agree to assist my mother safely out of the ghetto. Less than twenty-four hours later, we were kissing our excited and astonished relatives in Ostrowiec Świętokrzyski. We breathed deeply once more.

IV.

Ostrowiec Świętokrzyski - Extermination of the Jews

Ostrowiec Świętokrzyski was a small city. About 40% of its inhabitants were Jews, marked by the white armband with the blue Star of David. They worked as tailors, barbers, and craftsmen. The Jews even worked for the Germans, collecting wages for their work. We felt as though the gates of hell were behind us. My brother and father went to work at my uncle's barbershop, my mother and sister helped my aunt with the household chores, and I wandered idly between the house, the barbershop, and the streets, seeking some form of employment.

The relative peace was interrupted every so often, when the Jewish community was given some new order such as delivering, within twenty-four hours, two hundred fur coats, or so many pairs of shoes, or some sum or other of money or gold. The leaders of the community organized a "contributions" collection to assist Jews of differing financial situations. For this purpose, homes were visited and lists made of names and property. As Jewish refugees of another community, we were registered in the local records as longstanding citizens in the city. When the requirements were met, after much arguing and negotiating, the property was handed over to the Germans, and there resumed a period of relative calm.

Jews were out in the city and the surrounding towns and villages. An alternative market developed: clothes, shoes, housewares, and the like were traded for vegetables, poultry, and other farm produce. The state of peace persisted for several months, until suddenly a decree was issued, recruiting Jews to work for no pay. The Jewish area was designated a ghetto, and the city's Jews were forced to reside within it, although there were no walls or gates. Then, freedom of movement about the city was restricted; licenses to pass between areas were given only to those who worked for the Germans. The cost of food skyrocketed; again the Jews were not allowed to do business and any commodity of value had to be handed over to the Germans. Houses were searched, and people found hiding anything of value were dragged out into the streets in front of passersby. Again, my brother and I hired ourselves out to work in place of other Jews who still had money.

Recalling the situation in Warsaw, my uncle persuaded his friends in the Jewish community council to arrange permanent work permits for my father and I. We were both recruited to work in a German munitions factory in the city of Starachowice, about 30 km from Ostrowiec. This was considered to be the best work as it was steady, tantamount to insurance against deportation or other decrees.

The workers would gather at the train station where we were counted before going to the gates of the factory where, after a thorough search and examination, we were led by armed guards to our workplaces. We worked day and night shifts, mainly unloading boxes from the factory cars and loading them onto freight trains. I used to watch the loaded trains depart on their way, guessing at the amount of ammunition and what would be done with it. If only there was a way to sabotage them, to destroy the load or set it on fire—these were the thoughts that occupied my imagination. But in reality nothing could be done. We were well checked upon arrival and well supervised while we were working; we were forbidden to speak to one another. Work was quick and efficient—unload, load, unload, load—and the armed guards needed no pretext to open fire on the workers.

We worked like machines, and at the end of the shift we returned home completely shattered. The days passed, each the same as the next.

Before we left the Warsaw ghetto, I asked a Polish friend to inform the association as to the destination of our escape. I did not want to have simply disappeared without a word. I also knew that there were large forests sprawling around Ostrowiec, the Kielce forests, and rumor had it that there were partisans there. I requested that headquarters be informed that I would try to make contact with them.

One day as I was walking through the streets of Ostrowiec, a familiar-looking young man passed me. From his piercing gaze I saw that he knew me too. This was one of the operatives from the organization. Though previously we had not been good friends, here, far from Warsaw, we felt very close. We greeted one another and stood at the edge of the street, like people engaged in casual greeting. Briefly, he told me that he was with the partisans in the forest and had come to Ostrowiec to gather information about the German army in the vicinity. I told him that we worked in Starachowice, at the weapons factory that produced ammunition for cannons. I asked to join the partisans, but he rejected my request saying, enthusiastically, "You can be of much more use there... it will be very informative for the organization..."

We were careful not to speak too long in the street and set a daily meeting for ten in the morning. I was to wait beside the newspaper stand at the edge of the street and read the papers on display until he came. Then I would give him information about the factory. I was entrusted to inspect the factory and report on the guards' shifts and comings and goings at the gate. If he did not come I was to wait for him again the following day. For two days I waited in vain. On the third day he came, listened to what I had to say, and hurried away. Our allegiance gave new purpose to my life and I eagerly awaited our meetings. I also gathered information from workers in other places. I gave him brief reports so that I would not forget and to make it easier on him.

Then came the day that my friend appeared, very worked up. "Mjetek!" he said urgently, "Tell me quickly what you know and then leave the city. Go wherever you must, but do not stay here... I cannot take you with me..."

"Why?" I asked, "What happened?"

"Don't waste time!" He responded hurriedly. "Tomorrow there will be an action in your street."

"Action? In our street? In Ostrowiec? No—tomorrow is Saturday, the city will be quiet."

"Don't argue! Tell me what you brought, I have to go!"

I told him everything I knew and we quickly went our separate ways. I got home with my mind empty of thoughts. My father had not yet returned from his nightshift, which went until two in the afternoon. At one thirty, I would have to leave by train in a group of three hundred Jewish workers to replace the previous shift. I asked my mother to call my uncle and told them what I had heard. Shortly afterward, my uncle, my brother, and the neighbors were gathered in the room, and I repeated my announcement. I did not have details of what was going to happen, but we remembered the actions that had happened in Warsaw all too well... My uncle, the barber in whose shop many Germans, including high-ranking officials, had their hair cut, got angry and dismissed the rumor: "If something was expected to happen I would know about it!" He berated me. "Just today, three soldiers were at the shop and I did not feel anything was unusual!"

The others echoed my uncle's opinion.

"Don't stir up panic," my brother told me. "We would feel if there were special preparations happening. They wouldn't be able to hide something like that. In Warsaw, we always could tell..."

All of my protests, the credibility of my informant, and my fear did not help. Not one of them believed me and, to tell the truth, even I was not sure about the rumor. I decided to hide anyway, though I did not go too far.

"I will not go to work," I told myself, "and tomorrow I will not stay home."

I did not show up for work. In the evening I separated from my mother and brother thinking that they were right, that all my efforts were in vain, and who knows what harm I had done myself for not showing up! I went to Jurek, my Polish friend, who lived far from the ghetto. Everything was so calm and normal. Nobody stopped me in the street. There were no guards around the Jewish area. Jurek did not object to hosting me and did not even ask for an explanation.

In the early morning, we awoke to a strange noise. The muffled sounds were coming from loudspeakers some distance away. In a moment of shock, I realized that the rumor had been true... My friend and his parents sat beside me, their eyes filled with apprehension, afraid to look me in the eye. We were silent. We tried to make out what was being said over the loudspeakers. It was enough to hear "fast!" and "out!" to tell us what was happening.

That night the Germans had quietly surrounded the ghetto. In place of the missing walls and the open gates were masses of

Ukrainians, Germans, and Polish policemen, all of them armed. They made a huge ring around the Jewish streets, more effective than any wall. At five in the morning, the loudspeakers began to declare an order to register all those present in the ghetto. It was announced that immediately after listing the names, everyone would return home. There would be no need to bring anything except personal documents. Policemen and soldiers got everyone out of the houses. Many people, just woken from sleep and dressed in haste, gathered in the market square. Nobody noticed the train parked in the station at the square, until the police began to direct them aboard. Only then was there an outburst of screams. People began to grasp what was happening. Suppressed screams became wailing. Those who had work papers were herded into the communal buildings and guarded by armed Ukrainian soldiers.

While the cries were still being heard from the square, they began to build a temporary wall of boards, poles, and barbed wire around the fifteen or so community buildings. A ghetto within a ghetto was built, but this time it was a closed ghetto, with no way to leave. People darted towards the trains, requesting to join their families. Some tore up their work papers or handed them over to others and left to embrace their crying children. Many were in shock, separated from their families, shouting after them, "Don't worry, we will meet there!" Everything happened at a terrible speed, hurried along by shouting soldiers jabbing at people with the butts of their rifles, and behind them more soldiers, with their rifles aimed at the crowd, shooting from time to time at anyone who did not follow orders. Machine guns were stationed at the end of each street leading to the square.

We could hear the shots and the shouting from afar, but I only learned the details the following day. My friend and his parents did not say a word as I got dressed, my hands shaking. But when I went to leave, Jurek stopped me, saying, "Sit and wait here. You're not going anywhere right now!"

Jurek's mother made me something hot to drink but I was unable to touch it. I paced the room frantically as the sounds from the ghetto stabbed me like a sword.

When the sounds from the ghetto quieted, Jurek left the house, and returned much later, in the afternoon. According to him, many Jews remained in the tiny reduced ghetto and had even been joined by workers who had returned from the Saturday shift.

I decided to return to the ghetto. I realized that I had hidden in vain. I could not escape to the partisans as long as I did not know the fate of my family. I waited until evening and then crept back, this time to the new ghetto...

There were many Jews in the fifteen big buildings, including other workers that had been brought there from nearby. We assumed that the Germans had decided to concentrate the "useful" forces while separating the "non-useful." I met many acquaintances but to my great fear, I did not see anyone from my family. One acquaintance answered my questions in a dry, hollow voice, that they had all been taken. He went on to say that one officer of the Gestapo that used to have his hair cut at my uncle's shop, offered my sister to work for him in his household and to be spared the journey, but she had held on tight to my mother and refused. My mother, sister, uncle, and aunt along with our neighbor were together. When I asked about my brother who had a work permit, the man did not know what to tell me.

"I did not see him," he said.

"Maybe he went to work the Friday evening shift," I suggested hopefully. "And my father?"

I looked for my brother and father among those workers who had returned from shifts but I did not find them.

The pain was too great to bear. I moved through the crowd searching, searching in vain. "Mother..." I kept murmuring to myself, "Mother... Miraleh..." I sat in the corner of the courtyard and listened to the world beyond the ghetto. Voices could still be heard. From the silence, occasional shots and screams were heard, suggesting the discovery of those who had tried to hide. Time stretched on and the silence grew long. The houses were dark and empty. There was a suffocating feeling of lack of air, a feeling of unreality, as if everything was happening beyond us, at a distance. Everything had happened oo quickly. All at once, we were uprooted from our ordinary lives and thrown into a state of unreal horror. We sat where we were, unable to sleep.

Not a single German could be seen in the buildings' courtyards, as though they were afraid of how we would react and had left us alone to get used to the situation and understand that nothing could change the fact that we did not know the fate of our loved ones, and should we ever wish to find out, we would do our best to keep being quiet and useful...

For two days, all of our contact with the Germans consisted in receiving food. Only on the third day did commissars appear and begin to draw up new, updated lists for our work placements.

V.

The Iron Factory

I found my brother Yehezkel two months later. He was thinner, paler, and strange, but it was my brother, my brother Yehezkel, whom I thought I had lost. His hands grasped my shoulders in a spasm worse than words or explanation could describe, and his eyes bore into mine in disbelief. The meeting was sudden and caught me unprepared.

Three hours earlier we had been brought as a large group, evacuated from the ghetto, to the new camp beside the iron factory, where we had been working for the last two months. Many groups came, darting between the four big barracks designated as workers' quarters. Immediately upon our arrival, our group was put in formation, and remained so, standing for a long time, until they had arranged the others. The camp commander began with a speech, the likes of which we had already heard and would hear many times more. The essence of the speech was: "Here, in this camp named for Hermann Goering, you will live undisturbed. Here you will work for the Third Reich. You must give over any money in your possession, and anyone found with money will be killed immediately..."

We placed the small parcels that had accompanied us on our journey thus far on the ground. Ukrainian soldiers moved between us with sacks into which all of our valuables were gathered. My bundle was meager—I had come directly to the ghetto from my hiding place with nothing. I begged the man beside me in line to give me several of his bills so that I would have something to throw into the sack, in order to avoid special attention.

After further warnings from the German commander, the soldiers entered the empty barracks and searched them carefully. In one of the barracks, inside a bag of straw, several dollars were found. The commotion among the soldiers increased, and soon the "criminals" were found, two brothers that had arrived together. They were taken out in front of the formation. The commander's shrill voice demanded to know whose money it was—and a human drama unfolded before the hundreds of silent spectators. Both brothers shouted in unison, "The money is mine!" Their shouts, mixed with tears, pierced our hearts. The German was quiet for a while until his face twisted into a creepy smile, "Both of you are heroes, ah? Great. So come, both of you!" They were placed, sitting, with their heads to the fence, their hands together, until the gunshots put an end to their lives.

In the deep silence the German shouting was heard again, "This is what will happen to anyone who hides money, you hear? Do what you are told and you will not be punished!" Nobody moved until orders were given to disperse.

The practice of leading us to the barracks in a march had not yet been established. We were dismissed and in the chaos, as I was wondering which way to go, I suddenly found myself facing Yehezkel, my brother, who looked at me in astonishment... We fell into each other's arms, mumbling names and words. With trembling hands, my brother pulled me after him: "Mjetek, come, come Mjetek, let's move you into our barracks... I will arrange it... tell me... tell me something..."

We set down our straw sacks, meant for sleeping, side by side on the bunk and spoke. I told of Mother and Miriam, and Father—that I had not found him, nor anyone who had news of him. I told of the recent weeks, in which we were moved from one workplace to another until we got to the iron factory, and from there to here. Our stories were surprisingly similar, only the names of places were different.

On that same morning when the ghetto was evacuated, they were not sent home, but left at work, wondering and afraid to guess the reason. My brother remembered my warnings and repeated them to the others, but even then they refused to believe it. Yehezkel was sure that we were all lost and that he alone remained. When he suddenly saw me, he did not recognize me at first—I looked too old... the recent weeks had aged us both.

The small camp was next to the iron factory that produced the raw materials for making cannon parts. Most of the camp's prisoners worked in the factory. A few worked in other jobs in the city or its surroundings, such as digging drainage ditches. Both of us belonged to one group, though we were not always on the same shift. In the center of the factory, a huge oven built from large stones rose to a height of 25 meters, in which huge quantities of scrap iron was melted into medium sized bars which were then sent on to manufacture artillery pieces.

We worked beside and on top of the oven. Trolleys loaded with various iron scraps, broken iron tools and coal were brought to the oven. The workers attached the trolleys to lifts, which were raised onto the roof with a pulley. Eight local Christian workers that had been there since before the war worked up top. Some of the Jewish workers helped them, myself included.

On the roof platform was a large lid that was opened by pulling on a chain. After we had poured the contents of about thirty-five trolleys, loaded with iron bars, into the opening of the oven, we would close the lid. And while the workers below were increasing the heat, we would lower the empty trolleys and raise up full ones in preparation for the next melting phase.

The lower part of the oven had two openings: the upper opening was used to remove dirt and waste, and the lower opening poured the hot, liquid iron into dugout pits, whose walls were lined with boards to form casting molds. The iron would cool down in the pits, and when it hardened they would break it into bars, each three meters long. Other workers would then load the bars onto trolleys and send them to the nearby factory.

On the side of the oven were several chimneys that were closed with special windows. They were designed to clean the oven of the gases that formed inside while the fire was burning. The chimneys would be opened after the liquid iron had gone down and the pressure decreased. When it had cooled a bit, the chimneys were opened for ventilation, and at the same time we would add scraps from above. After we finished, everything would be closed and we would begin to light the oven again.

At the edge of the roof was a small tin hut, where the Polish workers lived. They were quite pleasant towards us, the Jewish workers, and I even had friendly relations with them, which was very useful to me throughout our work together. The work was carried out in three shifts, day and night, with no break. Between the sharp iron scraps jutting out from every direction, having to unload them, and the terrible heat coming from the oven, the work felt like a kind of hell, though our conditions were still better than those of the workers below.

The camp beside the factory was surrounded by several barbed wire fences. There was a guard tower in each of its four corners and a guard room beside the gate. Most of the guards were

Ukrainians. We walked to work in groups of 50 men each, escorted by policemen armed with machine guns and rifles. There were also policemen walking around the camp. But supervision of the workers on the way to and within the camp was not especially strict. It was possible, in various ways, to make connections with the local Polish farmers, and to trade a bit with them, which was how people from the camp usually managed to supplement the meager food rations. We received three meals a day: bread, jam, and coffee or tea in the morning and evening, and bread and a half liter of soup at midday. We were never full, but we were not meant to die of hunger. We secretly bought vegetables and other foods from the farmers.

Despite the searches, many people managed to hide money. We found money and things of value among the metal household goods that came along with the scrap iron from the areas of the Jewish evacuees. We were always amazed at the strange places that our lost brothers stashed money. Stories and legends emerged around the camp of treasures hidden in double bottoms, the handles and lids of pots and kettles, and we spent a good deal of time searching. Sometimes we hid small household items that were still useable and traded them for food. Life went on with some degree of routine, with each man free to his own thoughts, concerns, and memories...

VI.

Man in the Iron Furnace

On Christmas Eve at the end of 1943, I was working the night shift, and the Polish workers were in a pretty good mood. They had brought cakes and drinks and were taking advantage of the short ceasefire to celebrate their holiday. They gave me a slice of cake and I remember that I held it for a while before eating it, recalling my mother's house. Suddenly, without warning or preparation, a terrible explosion was heard. The electricity went out and the world seemed to have returned to chaos—all at once waves of intense heat flooded the small hut.

We dashed towards the door and were greeted by a hot cloud of fire, smoke, and the strong smell of burning. To our great horror, we saw that the lid of the oven was completely crushed, and a flow of melted iron, like a stream of lava, was rising up within it and flowing onto the roof, splattering and spreading sparks and burning gas all around. The walls of the hut, made from tin about 5 millimeters thick, glowed red.

The workers shouted, "Quick! To the stairs!" I saw them jump over the molten iron towards the stairs. I dashed after them, but to my great misfortune I forgot about the trolley tracks running the length of the roof. I tripped over them and fell into a puddle of burning iron... I heard gruesome sounds and I knew that my flesh had burned. I rose and continued, blindly groping my way towards the stairs. I found myself steadying my legs on the impossibly hot iron steps, descending slowly.

My face and hands were badly burnt. When I tripped, I had instinctively broken my fall with my hands, which bore most of the injury. This had prevented the boiling liquid touching my face and protected my eyes, but the sides of my face and my hair had not been spared. The flesh hung and disintegrated into pieces and my clothes were smoking. People looked at me in horror and were afraid to come near me. Amazingly, my mind was fully aware despite the terrible pain that had begun to assault my senses and nerve centers. I knew that there was an oil bucket nearby, in which we oiled the trolley wheels. I searched for it, through teary eyes, and found it. I thrust both my hands into the bucket up to my elbows, gripped by nausea. I felt my face burning with pain, but I still did not know its actual state.

Suddenly I heard a hesitant and fearful voice ask, "Mjetek, is that you? What happened?" As if through a fog, I recognized the voice of Isser, one of my old friends from Ostrowiec, who had been with us all this way on our tortuous journey. He worked below, in the office, and had heard the explosions. He knew that I was above, and amid the commotion, had suddenly seen me. He was seized with panic at the sight of me... In that moment I could not remember what had happened. Only afterward, I understood that he had led me to the factory's first aid station.

One medic fainted at the sight of me while the Polish medic stood at a loss, not knowing what to do. Isser quickly recovered from his shock and, feeling responsible for me in the absence of my brother, called out urgently, "Come, Mjetek, we will run to the doctor at the camp!" When I did not answer, he dragged me after him, running, and I stumbled along after him, stunned...

We reached the guard post. The whole way, Isser was crying out, evidently to guards who leaped towards him, "To the doctor! We are running to the doctor!" Amid waves of unconsciousness, some voices permeated, and I heard the sound of a weapon. The guard looked at me up close and it was as good as any document. The gate opened before us. Later, Isser described to me how I had looked: blackened and burnt clothes, with burnt skin poking out here and there, and black and red flesh, my face burnt and gaping eyes staring out—no wonder the Ukrainian guard did not even ask a single question...

Luckily for me, there were no German guards at the gate just then, because it was not time for a shift change, and the camp was under the darkness of night. The Germans were busy with the big explosion, and amid the great commotion, only a few people noticed my arrival, mainly Jews. Hearing Isser's calls, they quickly alerted my brother. I was brought to the aid hut. The doctor, a Jew from Germany, immediately responded,

"The arms must be cut off, otherwise he'll die!"

Then his helper stepped forward and said in a slow and clear voice, that still rings in my ears, "We must *not* cut off the hands or he will certainly die!" And he ran his hand across his neck, gesturing a slaughtering motion.

The hint was understood by all—a prisoner in a work camp with no hands is not long for this world—as it was my life and safety were hardly guaranteed and crucially, if the camp commander or his aides were to see me they would certainly spare the medical treatment and save me from my misery quickly and with German efficiency. Meanwhile, I collapsed onto the bed, overwhelmed by waves of pain.

My pain grew unbearable. The doctor gave me a double shot of morphine and I sank into a blessed state of numbness.

Only much later was I told by Yehezkel and Isser what had happened to me then. Ohelmann, the doctor's assistant, was a Jewish barber from Ostrowiec and a friend of my father. He was granted his position as a medic on account of his one year of training as a medical student. Already in Ostrowiec, he was known for his treatments, such as blood-letting, using cupping glasses, and the like.

Ohelmann pulled the doctor aside and spoke to him in a whisper. Afterward he told my brother that he had asked him for another day or two to take care of me in his way, and not to report it to the Germans. He promised the doctor that if the Germans were to find out, he would say that he alone had treated me and that the doctor had not even known of my injury. He further reasoned that the Germans were busy investigating the explosion and fixing the damage, seeing to the workers and imposing order and that they might not hear of my injury for some time yet. The doctor finally agreed, and left the hut mumbling and sighing, approving another shot of morphine for me when I woke up.

That night, my brother Yehezkel took all the window panes out of the hut in which I might have seen my reflection. He worried that I would see my face and despairing, hand myself over to the Germans.

My first treatment was carried out while I was still unconscious. Ohelmann recruited another Jewish medic named Gottholz to help him, and together, the two of them set about the task at hand—a desperate battle for my life and survival. It seemed as though saving my life had become a cause for the camp, for all of Jewish existence—saving the life of one man within this hell of death and terror, in the hands of the Germans. After washing my burns with quicklime, they applied masks and bandages of oil... there were no other medicines. Even oil was scarce, and friends bought it from Poles in town for high prices. Whole liters of oil in different forms were smuggled into the camp, at risk of death. From time to time, Jews came in to see me—some were friends and acquaintances and others were strangers trying to make the visit without arousing any attention.

My status and progress was the subject of conversation in camp. Volunteers would come to help change bandages—a terrible task, which required strong nerves. My flesh gave off a strong stench and would stick to the bandages, peeling off in layers as they were removed. The pain was terrible but the doctor refused to increase the dose of morphine. Each change of bandages was a major lesson for everyone involved. Food was also brought to me from the camp. I was not able to chew, and I drank the soup and the tea through a glass tube. My lips were scorched and scarred and even sucking caused me pain.

I lay like a rock in that narrow bed for four months. Slowly I was able to get up, make several rounds about the room, and return to my bed. My "doctors" insisted that I walk and get used to my legs and arms, to avoid atrophy from constant lying down. Four months passed before I recovered and returned to work.

To this day, I cannot get over how unbelievable this all was—four months of convalescing in a German work camp, without the Germans knowing or finding out. I believe that this was possible on account of a combination of lucky circumstances: the sentry by whom we had initially passed did not report anything, perhaps he thought I was dead anyway. Certainly the chaos of the fire added to the general confusion. The Germans suspected, probably rightly so, that the explosion was the result of sabotage at the factory. It turned out that the ventilation windows had not been opened and the gases accumulated in the bottom of the oven so that as the fire continue to burn with no release, they were further compressed, pushing the iron upward with extreme force until the lid exploded and the molten iron burst upward like a pillar of lava, in fire and smoke. An investigation was carried out, and many of the workers were not seen on the grounds again. The Germans announced, with their particular brand of sarcasm, that those responsible would not be able to repeat any such act, or any act at all, and the same would go for any future offenders. In the confusion, searches, and investigations, my injury went unnoticed and I was saved.

But above all, I owe the miracle of my not being discovered to my friends—those familiar to me and those I never knew—who took care of me in my state and took unspeakable pains to obtain the oil to heal my wounds and save me some of their meager rations. They took turns, working in my place, in addition to their own work so that the supervisors would not notice my absence. Out of all of them, only my friend Isser remains alive, among us today. The others were lost.

When the bandages were first removed from my face, I stared at myself in the mirror that Yehezkel brought, and fainted! My face was a mask of shiny, red flesh, with a pair of eyes flashing from within, and a nose sticking out. Eventually, the red faded and returned to the right color. I was saved from permanent scarring by the fact that my face had been protected by my hands when I fell. The scars on my hands remain to this day, and for a long time, made working difficult.

With the help of my brother and friends, I was appointed "deputy foreman," second in command to the group leader. This way I did not have to work too much with my hands. I went about between the workers and tried not to be seen by the Germans. We sewed a pair of gloves from rags so I could keep my hands bandaged until they were completely healed and I was, once again, like everybody else.

VII.

The Uprising That Failed

It was August of 1944. There were excited rumors in the air of the Russians approaching, and every day there was more hearsay and "announcements." One day I was working the morning shift. Suddenly, around ten o'clock, a siren was heard, and the factory speakers directed group leaders to gather all the Jewish workers and return immediately to the camp.

We stopped working. The factory went quiet. We were stunned—the second shift had not yet arrived, but we were being called back to camp—what did it mean? Nobody said aloud what we all feared, but it pierced our hearts, knowing what we had experienced so far. Some claimed that they were evacuating the camp because of the approaching Russians. People began to conspire: to escape... to hide... to wait...

Isser Gerber appeared beside me and cried, excitedly, "Mjetek, you know what? Come let's hide among the scrap metal. We will wait for the Russians. What do we have to lose?"

I agreed, but immediately answered, "But Yehezkel is at the camp! If he comes with us... we will escape. If not—I must return to camp..."

I approached the first group that was heading to the camp and asked someone I knew to tell Yehezkel to come to the factory any way he could. I waited a while, until the police returned to take the second group. One of the Jewish supervisors that had come back with them brought me a message from my brother: the gate is closed, there is no way out. The entire camp was surrounded by armed guards standing ten meters apart and soldiers with dogs patrolling the grounds...

Isser implored me to stay and hide, saying that within just a few days the Russians would come and we would be released and could join their army... I wanted nothing more, but how could I leave my brother behind? After all the hardship we had endured together, his immense devotion to me in the months when I had lain bedridden, being the last remaining members of our family... Isser bade me goodbye and disappeared. I was among the last to return to the camp.

Later we heard that most of the people that had tried to hide were caught in their hiding places and killed on the spot. I mourned Isser and tormented myself for letting him take that risk.

Only after the war was over, when I met Isser, shocked with happiness, did I hear his tale of what happened: he was well-hidden, silent and still; he heard the Germans shooting and the screams of those who were killed; it took all his might to survive the unbearable hunger, knowing that if he left his hiding place or was found he would die. When the area was completely quiet, he fled to the neighboring town, where there were farmers who used to trade with his father. They agreed to hide him, believing, as he had convinced them, that the Russians were close and would reward them for their deeds. When the Russian army arrived, Isser volunteered to join up and serve as a regular soldier.

I returned to the camp and when I saw Yehezkel's pale face glowing when he saw me, I was glad I had decided to return. He embraced me wordlessly, as if to say they will not separate us...

We were instructed to pack our things and be ready to go. We stood in the assembly yard, awaiting further instruction. Captain Zbaydjina, the camp commander, appeared, stepped up on the small stage and made a speech, the essence of which was: "Do not panic... the front is coming this way and we wish to save you... we will send you to Germany where you will work and live as you lived here, and perhaps it will even be better. You are our workers and we are looking after you..." The captain finished his speech and left, and chaos descended upon the yard. Many were in disbelief. The feeling in the air was that this was the end.

One of the most worked up among us was Gottholz the medic, who was largely responsible for saving my life. He was agitated, talking about the craftiness of the Germans, their artful lies and the unthinkable horrors that they hid beneath their smooth talk. He recalled the evacuation of the city ghetto, the rumors of the end met by those families that were taken. He began to elaborate on his own idea, beginning with musing on a daring plan of action, thrilling in its intensity: "Friends!" cried Gottholz, and his eyes lit up. "Comrades, we can do something... there are so many of us... we can attack the Ukrainians, by surprise, all together, shouting... we can grab their weapons... some will have to shoot, to cover one another, or be shot as we flee... we will escape to the woods and scatter," he said, spreading his arms wide as though he were embracing the world around him. "We will hide in the woods and wait for the Russians... surely many people will die, but we will die anyway, all of us... this way some of us may be saved!" His whole body shook with excitement, and he gazed at those around him.

The people looked at him with an astonishment mix of admiration and fear. Voices shouted, "Really, *now*, when our liberation is so close? It is not worth endangering our lives. They will overpower us... we want to see our families again... they will not manage to transfer us. The army has withdrawn, the roads are blocked..." Another was heard in a hushed voice, "I don't even know how to use a gun..."

Ultimately, in the ensuing uproar, many jumped to carry out Gottholz's plan. Of all the men who decided to take the risk, four survived and fled the camp, Gottholz among them.

We were distressed seeing the bodies of our brave friends, some of whom hung from the barbed wire fence and others scattered around in puddles of blood. There was silence. Our hearts leaped with fear for the four who had escaped, and we prayed that they would find their way. For several hours we remained, standing, surrounded by armed guards with a murderous look in their eyes until a group of German soldiers showed up dragging a horrible cargo: four men tied tight with blood pouring from their awful wounds. They had been caught some distance from the camp, where they had hidden in the field. The woods were too far, and the dogs too fast...

The Ukrainian commander, tall and threatening, brought Gottholz and the others to the platform in the yard. We stood silently, our legs failing from standing the entire punishing time, waiting. The man approached Gottholz and said angrily, "You, you deserve a bullet in the head... you thought you could escape?"

The wounded Gottholz stared at him and answered quietly, "A bullet to the head? You don't have it in you!"

We were filled with terror. Why was he taunting him and why would he bring on his own death?

The Ukrainian answered, "You do not believe? Watch!" He pulled out his gun and aimed it at Gottholz. In the blink of an eye, Gottholz leaped up and, as we held our breaths, grabbed the Ukrainian's hand, fighting him for the gun... The big, strong Ukrainian began shouting, "Help! Help!"

None of the soldiers dared to shoot Gottholz for fear of hurting their commander. The twenty guards quickly pointed their weapons at the people around, so that none could come to Gottholz's aid. At the same time, three guards surrounded the two men fighting, and one of them gave our friend a crushing blow to the head. He fell to the ground and the Ukrainian shot him six times, one after the other. The Ukrainians joined him, shooting into the air. This caused great commotion, sending people running to the barracks and many were hit by the shots. One of my friends, Lazar, disoriented, ran towards the guard who aimed his gun and shot him. The bullet went in through one cheek and came out the other, leaving him shrieking but alive...

All that time, Gottholz lay in the yard. The Germans chose a few of us to bury him. The grave was dug beside the fence, big enough to include the friends that had escaped with him. I approached his body, I do not know why. I knew that this was dangerous, since it might arouse the suspicion of the guard standing nearby. In any case, I approached. Maybe I wanted to give him some final respect, or to apologize, without words, for disappointing him and not joining his cause. I looked into his face, filled with blood, and for a shocking moment, I saw his eyes slowly open and look at me. I felt my blood turn to ice but did not move. Careful not to make any hasty movements, I whispered to one of the gravediggers, "Yurek, he's alive! Gottholz is alive! I saw his eyes move! What should we do?"

Yurek looked at me in shock but whispered back, "Come, dig and we will put him in the grave. We will cover him but leave a hole to breathe. Maybe he will stay alive until all of us are able to leave..."

This was more delusion than faith. He had been shot with six bullets when he was already wounded. How would he get out and how could he live? But we left him an opening anyway. Silently, I leaned over and cleared away the dirt with my hands. But suddenly one of the Ukrainian guards watching over us approached. Evidently, he understood the unlikely situation and a cruel smile lit up his face. "He's alive? No problem. We will bury him alive..."

A second guard, also Ukrainian, came to see what was happening. He was less cruel, and from time to time it was said that he took mercy, and even helped Jews. In his eyes he had compassion and a hint of admiration for Gottholz. Evidently, he made a decision then because the moment his friend turned his back, he raised his rifle and shot the dying man in the head. To his friend's cries, he replied, "He was getting up... I panicked and shot him."

We were not angry. We knew that he had done this out of mercy for our friend's suffering, and we continued our burial work with heads bowed.

The preparations to leave the next day made everything feel like some alternate universe. The gates of abundance opened and we were inundated with "gifts." We received an entire loaf of bread each and a packet of margarine, a sight we had not seen since our arrival at the camp. Everyone received a packet of jam. We were asked to bring the work tools that were distributed among us, as we would need them at the next work camp and we were permitted to bring along personal items.

Despite the horrors of the day before, here and there were faces smiling with hope. "The Germans are afraid of the Russians," people ruminated aloud hopefully, and "that's why they are behaving well... besides, they need us..." There is no end to man's naivety. He sees what he wishes to see, rather than reality. And reality was revealed, even to the innocents among us, very quickly.

We boarded the freight cars, well equipped, and soon began to feel the terrible congestion. About sixty men were crammed into each car, and the doors were locked from outside. The small windows were lined with metal bars. The train started on its way and morale began to plummet. It was uncomfortable. It was hot and airless. We did not receive water. For the first two days or so, we ate our fill. The train would stop for long stretches at the various stations, clearing the tracks for other trains. By the third day, there was no food left. Thirst ate away at our innards, and between the load of work tools and the bundles of clothes, some of us began to faint.

The Ukrainian guards sat on the car roofs and passed their time with pleasantries. They listened to the people pleading, "Water! Water!" and watched as they tried to buy water from the Poles at the train stations. They also observed the attempts to escape on the way, when planks were removed from the floors of the carriages, and from time to time we heard shots. Eventually they informed us that if someone escaped, they would kill all the people in the train car. That way they ensured we would be guarded from the inside as well as out.

VIII.

Auschwitz

Finally the train stopped. The large sign read "Auschwitz." All we knew about Auschwitz was that it was a tough work camp. We did not know anything else about the place. We remained locked inside the train cars until the next morning. Those closer to the windows looked out and described what they saw: a big camp, surrounded by many fences. Many Germans. We heard voices and orders in German coming closer, then the door opened. The first thing we saw were German soldiers holding whips, commanding us, "Get down... fast... run..." we got off. Fast. Anyone who delayed so much as a moment was hurried along with a snap of the whip. We were driven a considerable distance, still holding our work tools and bundles. Men were running, as were the women and children who had come off other train cars. The running did not permit us a moment to look around or think.

We got to a large wall lined by Germans sitting alongside armed soldiers. At the center of the wall, above the gate was the huge inscription "Work will set you free." The orders did not stop as we ran towards them, "Men to the right, women and children to the left!" The rushing, sometimes faltering queue split in different directions, and there was no time to consider what any of this meant... Everything was happening so quickly that there was not even time to feel the pain of separation. Out of the corner of my eyes, I saw mothers holding the hands of their children, hurrying them along, and men waving and calling out, "See you at the camp!"

It was like an active labor camp, maintaining efficiency, order, and speed. The line of men went through the gates, while the line of women and children turned the other way. We passed the wall, ran and stumbled until we reached an empty lot where we were ordered to stand. Many of us, exhausted, fell helplessly to the ground. After several minutes of rest, we received brief instructions to lay our things down in rows, march forward, and organize ourselves into straight lines of five. Armed guards surrounded the long lines and an officer passed through the groups of five, counted ten of them, and fifty men were marched toward the nearby barracks. We looked around at where we were and saw a long line of barracks surrounded by a fence of thick electric wire. The line stood still, each man waiting for his turn to move. We stood for a very long time, and eventually we too were marched towards a barracks. Order was maintained with the whistling of the whips and the shouting of the guards. We passed between barracks and saw the life of the camp from up close: busy prisoners hurried about, bringing food, running, calling to one another. We tried to ask them questions, ignoring the whips flying over our heads, but they did not answer or even stop what they were doing.

As we walked through the closely guarded gates, we saw more and more barracks surrounded by fences: camps within camps within camps, which seemed to stretch on forever. From time to time we heard shots from somewhere. We kept on walking, thinking of our bundles, which remained in that increasingly distant lot, which we would not likely find our way back to. We ruminated on a great many things until we got to a very small camp: two large, long barracks, similar in shape, with chimneys rising above them. Some distance from these, the barbed wire fences continued, rising to a height of about two and a half meters, connected to concrete poles, and white connectors indicating that the fence was thoroughly electrified.

The guards led us past these buildings—and for the first time since our arrival we heard screams and were alarmed; the screams announced bits of information. "They will burn us! Gas! Murder! Do not go in!" But of course their shouts did not help us. Who knows how many fences and gates and camps were all around us—guarded, surrounded, and defended. Where would we run to? The guards' shots and the crack of their whips "helped" us to decide—we marched towards the barracks...

To our great relief we found ourselves in a large hall, about twelve meters long. Along the walls were piles of various clothes and objects. At the end, on a wooden platform, stood a German officer with a gun and a whip. He announced, "You are now entering into an orderly work schedule. You will receive clothes and equipment; nothing is private here!" We were ordered to take off our clothes, march toward the wall, and put our clothes in piles: the whites in the white piles, the shirts in the shirt piles, and so forth.

We exited the building, naked as the day we were born, and immediately entered the second barracks. The inside was divided into rooms with narrow corridors between them, like on a train. In the first room there were maybe twenty people sitting, dressed in striped clothes like pajamas—like those worn by the prisoners outside. In their hands were strange shavers, with no water or soap. We were brought before them, each in front of a prisoner-barber, and watched by armed guards.

We were shaved down to the root of every hair on our bodies, without water or soap. To my amazement, I realized that images from the past flooded my memory, as if real, before my eyes: my father shaving one of his customers, putting a dollop of foam on his chin and speaking to him pleasantly...

The dry, dull shaver ripped the hair out cruelly, as if with an agenda of its own. Along with the hairs, bits of skin and flesh were torn off, and terrible shrieks of pain filled the room, mixing with the shouting of the guards, "Quickly! Quickly!" From there we passed through a narrow corridor to the next room. Just inside was a kind of makeshift bathtub, dug out from the earth. Each of us was forced in up to his knees in a disinfectant substance that emitted a strong smell, perhaps Lysol. Beside the bath stood a prisoner holding a rod wrapped in a dirty rag. He dipped the rag into the disinfectant and wiped us down with it quickly, under the arms, between the legs, and on the head. Any wounds burned and stung. People tried to escape to the sides, but the guards and their whips drove us through...

The strange barracks had not yet been used to their fullest—we passed through an iron door into yet another room, and the door closed behind us. The room was bare and empty, with strange trenches on the floor and small holes here and there. We glanced upwards—on the ceiling were openings, resembling a shower, from which came hot steam. Cries of pain were replaced by cries of terror—people wailed and shouted—but this was not the mysterious gas, which several of us had already heard about. After the steam subsided, water began to flow out, boiling water. We tried to shrink, to escape, to save our tender skin from burns— but by the time the water stopped we were all well washed, as the room was locked and the water came from every direction...

The door opened and, stunned, we stepped out. It seemed like a journey through hell—with no way back and no contact with those that remained behind. Only forward—and the future held horrific surprises. To our great relief, it seemed as though this agonizing chapter was over. Lines of prisoners wearing their striped clothes stood beside piles of clothes of a different sort: the striped pajamas, hats, camp sandals made from several layers of cloth, battered tin bowls and mugs; we passed with an outstretched hand, quickly receiving one of each item, like an assembly line.

We were given three minutes to put the clothes on our scorched bodies and then—even then—checks began: whether the clothes fit, who had new clothing and whose was old and torn; sizes were exchanged. How amazing is the power of existence in man—when we left the building to the lot, identical to one another in our astonishing ugliness, we found before us many groups similar to ours, sitting on the ground and on the grass that sprouted out here and there. We were led to a long wooden table, next to which stood five prisoners behind big pots; each of us held out his bowl to receive the thin, hot soup—with a command to finish drinking it within one minute. Whoever did not finish must dump out whatever remained. We drank. Those who did not finish—the thin liquid was hot—had the soup spilled from between his hungry lips with a lash of the guard's stick.

We were led through more gates and fences. We were thinking about torture and of the end, and these thoughts weighed on us more and more with each passing moment. Eventually, we were not thinking of anything except to put our exhausted heads down and sleep. Finally, we stopped next to a camp of ten long barracks surrounded, as always, by fences. We stopped beside the path and were ordered to sit on the ground, in the same order in which we had been walking, without scattering or moving. The guards kept a close eye on us as we carried out the order.

We laid our heads down on our knees. We sat that way for a long time. There were no clocks, but the day was passing and we knew that we sat there for a number of hours. All the while our eyes anxiously followed what the Germans were doing, evacuating the camp on the other side of the fence. It was a camp of gypsies—men, women, children, and elderly people—whole families still together, dressed in the colorful clothes particular to them, blurs of color in a black-and-white world... The evacuation took them by surprise, without warning. They were shrieking and screaming, some struggling and trying to fight the guards who smiled at them mercilessly, dragging and even shooting some of them. Finally, silence prevailed, broken only by bitter wailing as the long lines got farther and farther away beyond the fence.

Afterward, we were told that the gypsies were led to the gas chambers and crematorium. Clearing the camp of its residents continued until late into the night. Several of us fell into a strange slumber, twitching sporadically, tormented by dreams. Others stared blankly out of empty faces. Some time later the sounds of the guards shouting returned and we were woken and led to the camp. About four hundred men were brought to each barracks, standing beside one another crammed together waiting... In the middle of the barracks was a sort of stove made of burnt bricks, that continued the entire length of the building, but the stove was out and cold. Otherwise the place was empty. The space still bore the smell of its previous occupants, and it was as if they were eying us with silent fury... Here and there were small items, forgotten in the chaos of the evacuation. From time to time someone would bend over and hide something in his clothes.

The kapo entered, a tall, broad-shouldered Pole, grasping a thick stick in his hands. He got up on the stove and walked to the center of the barracks where he stood, legs apart, shaking his stick, and roared out to the hundreds of crowded and nervous men, casting his cruel gaze at the guards standing by the entrance with their weapons pointed at us. His speech this time was different than what we had grown accustomed to hearing. Without introduction, he began, "You did not come here to work! You will only be here for a few days, and then you will go the same way as those that were here before you!" He gestured to the barracks with a sweeping motion. "There is only one way out of here—through the chimney..." He looked at us with a smile but not one of us uttered a word. I glanced at my brother standing beside me; he had a tortured look on his face. We were quiet. The man continued, "You have no need for anything. If someone has money or gold—give it to me. I will give him some bread for it—that he may have provisions on his way to Moshe Rabeinu..." If he expected some smile for his special sense of humor, he was certainly disappointed. Suddenly, he shouted out, "Lie down!" We looked at one another in dread. We were so cramped standing—how would we find space to lie down? Commotion ensued to which he responded by shouting and waving his cane. The armed guards entered the fray, also standing on the burnt red bricks, and waiting attentively. But the kapo managed just fine without any help from them. He pushed those standing before him to one side of the barracks. Then he called us to him one by one. The first lay down with his head towards the wall. The second pressed against him with his head toward the stove. And so forth, he directed several more to lie down, waving his cane and shouting. Eventually all of us were lying down, squashed together, unable to move. The barracks floor was completely covered without an inch of empty space.

The kapo had not yet exhausted his special sense of humor. He got down off the stove and began to walk over bodies, stepping on various organs without notice. Each yelp or movement was met with the cruel beatings from the kapo's cane. He then shouted at us again to hand over any gold or money, and with his disappointment grew his blows and kicks.

The screams were terrible to hear—and all the while the guards did not move. This was, apparently, an additional exercise in our training. When the kapo finally left us, exiting the barracks, the guards disappeared too. We were no longer any real threat to them.

In the morning, when we awoke, there were cries of alarm—some of the men were found dead. The kapo's kicks and blows were well aimed. He clearly knew that in advance because just then prisoners appeared, dragging carts to carry away the dead.

IX.

Blacksmith at the Buna Monowitz Camp

We continued in the same way for five days. We received food once a day: a bowl of "soup" of murky water. We did not work. From the morning until the evening we were kept occupied with various tasks: cleaning, running, sitting without moving, gymnastics. In the evening we were brought into the barracks and forced to lie down beside each other in complete silence until the morning. The sound of a sigh was enough to bring the kapo forth from his room at the far side of the barracks and deliver beatings left and right.

We spent the day making attempts to communicate with one another through whispers and gestures. Other prisoners who had been there for some time would trade scraps of bread with one another, even the kapo. Everything was under the radar, such that the guards would not notice. Where people got money from—we could not understand. From time to time we succeeded in having short conversations in which we shared what was on our minds. Hope was scarce. We were in a strange state of mind—a kind of petrification of the brain, rejecting thoughts, similar to hypnosis. We would walk about and look at one another, our minds completely empty. My brother and I were encouraged by the fact of being together. We were careful not to speak to one another for fear of being separated. We were satisfied with a glance or a touch of the hand, as if by accident.

At noon on the fifth day, there was a buzz of something happening in the camp. We saw people talking and others moving hurriedly. It was being said that whoever wished to work would have to stand in line to sign up. Anything was better than life in the camp. I called to my brother and we joined the line, standing one behind the other, pretending to be strangers. We stood there for a long time.

One after another, each man entered the office; beside a table sat two Germans and several prisoners. The old and the weak among us were led aside and taken away by the guards. The Germans wrote down our names and asked a few questions: past place of residence, age, details about the family and finally—profession. My brother answered, "barber" and I, young and without a profession, answered, for some reason, "blacksmith." Blacksmith work seemed simple to me, enough so that I could probably fake it, plus I knew that the Germans needed this kind of work. The man eyed me suspiciously and asked, "How is it that you are a blacksmith. You're young." I replied that my father and my grandfather were blacksmiths and I had worked with them since childhood. He hesitated for a moment, then wrote beside my name: "Blacksmith." I walked on without looking at my brother, lest my expression or his betray us.

After the registration, every man received a slip of paper with a number written on it. With the paper in hand, we moved right, where people were sitting by a small table, tattooing the number onto the forearm of the new "workers." They were holding a device similar to a fountain pen and copied the number that was written on the slip of paper onto each man's arm. At the end of the pen was a strange needle with which they stabbed the arm, inserting dye under the skin. With those tiny dots, they marked us irreversibly and each of us became a number, with which he would be identified from now on. There was instant swelling and redness. It hurt terribly. But we were well-schooled in suffering by now, and it was all done incredibly fast.

From there we were led to assemble. For hours we stood and waited. In the evening a group of Germans appeared, armed and accompanied by dogs. We were organized into groups of five and walked out of the camp on foot. We did not need any words of farewell. The farther we got, the lighter the load that we felt. We left Auschwitz without looking back. We walked and walked. Our group numbered three hundred and fifty men.

We were led through a small city. The city was under curfew and was dark and quiet. Armed Germans lined the streets and many of them held large dogs on chains. We did not see a single citizen. They did not even peer through the windows. Evidently they were not curious about the nighttime passersby. We left the city and walked on and on. After hours of grueling walking, without rest, with the first light of morning, we passed a huge building that looked like a factory, to the side of which were what appeared to be barracks, surrounded by electric wire fencing and guard towers.

This was Buna Monowitz camp, they told us the following day, a side camp of Auschwitz, where the factory's workers lived. "Buna" was not small—it held an estimated ten thousand men. Beside the entrance were the offices; farther beyond the gate was a stage on which the prisoners' orchestra played.

As we became acquainted with the camp and its residents, we came to learn that the orchestra members were among the best musicians in the world—prisoners like us, who found themselves in a German labor camp...

We were led to the barracks, with three levels of wooden

bunks, two men to each bunk. Here too it was very crowded. When it began to get cold, the crowding was beneficial since we were able to draw some warmth from one another. Again I managed to be with my brother since we pretended to be strangers and were beside one another as if by accident.

It was forbidden to leave the barracks at night. In the middle of the space were buckets for relieving oneself, and two prisoners were appointed to empty them each night. They would walk to the toilets accompanied by a guard who afterward returned them to the barracks.

Each barracks had its own "block elder," as it was called, and he had two assistants, "house helpers," who would maintain order and cleanliness in the barracks.

The following morning, after a short assembly, we were led to the showers to wash. There we received different clothes—still the same strange "pajamas" but clean and disinfected. The showers also had hot water. We were allotted a short amount of time and we showered quickly. There was no soap and no towels, so we put our clothes on our wet bodies. The clothing was: shirt, pants, wooden shoes, and a cloth jacket. Along with this we received a cloth "Star of David" in which the top part was red and the bottom part yellow; this we attached to the jacket. These were the markings of the camp. We learned that the red was a "political" marking and the yellow was "Jewish." So we were "Jewish-political" prisoners.

We quickly learned the rest of the markings: green—criminal prisoners, their symbol was just one triangle and not a Star of David, as they were not Jews. The red triangle marked the political prisoners and the black triangle was for those that were imprisoned for not participating in the war effort, "lazy dodgers," as they were nicknamed by the Germans. A purple triangle was the sign of the homosexuals, and so on. This way, we could tell from a distance what "crime" each man was guilty of...

Soon we knew that we could get along best with the "reds." The "greens" were mostly sadists, abusing everyone as though taking revenge on the entire human race; and these were the ones who primarily held the roles of kapo, block leader, and other positions. The Germans were good at choosing dedicated workers. The political prisoners, the "reds," were generally pleasant, and those of them who served various positions would not abuse the other prisoners.

We were divided into groups according to our skills. For each group, that is to say, for every profession, a leader was appointed, and called "the profession commando." After two weeks, we were assigned living quarters according to our "profession commando"—three to four work groups to a barracks. So, for the first time, I was separated from my brother, although we knew we would still see each other, as we were not far away.

I was sent to block 25. The block elder was Czech, wearing the red triangle, that is, a political prisoner, and was a kind man. I was in a state of anxiety; I knew what would happen to me if the Germans found out I had lied to them, and I did not know the first thing about metalwork. I did not talk to my neighbors, my fellow blacksmiths. They were all complete strangers to me and I was worried about disclosing my secret.

The day came when we went to work. The kapo set the pace of the walk. We marched past the main gate guarded by the kapo's men, the block elders and their helpers. Armed with canes, they made sure we marched as ordered, "Left, right!" From time to time they delivered a blow to those that stepped with the wrong foot.

In this manner, we quickly learned our walking order. In the coming days, we got into formation on our own, such that the young among us walked at the edges of the group, and the older or weaker walked in the middle, where the risk was diminished, especially once we saw that blows would be given even if there had been no mistakes in marching...

Our commando was immediately taken to the factory's carbide division. A kapo came to take us from the entrance and placed us at our jobs one by one. I was taken to the forge since I had declared myself a blacksmith. I entered the long hall. Alongside the machines worked Russian prisoners from nearby POW camps in ragged, worn out army uniforms. Many pairs of eyes followed our entrance.

The S.S. officer who headed the smithy sized me up from head to toe with disgust. I did not return his gaze with defiance or rebellion, nor even meet his eyes. "You are a blacksmith?" He asked. "You know how to work? What do you know to do?" The many questions made it easier to answer.

"I can do any smith work, Sir!" I answered with confidence, as if I myself believed what I was saying. I knew that my life depended on this, and I would not give myself up.

The man hummed, shaking his cane back and forth. "Well, let's see. Make me lilies." I was silent. What could I say?

"Lilies," he continued, "for the garden gate. Understand? I will come collect it in the evening. If the lilies are not pretty..." He did not continue but pushed his cane to my throat until I nearly choked. I understood. I mumbled, with difficulty, "Yes, sir... Tonight you will have very pretty lilies..."

The cane poked my shoulder, pushing me backward. "You've got yourselves a new blacksmith..." He spit finally, and with a light hit of the cane to my shoulder, walked away. I was left standing in front of the kapo, with the red triangle declaring him to be a German prisoner. He gestured to one of the worker-prisoners, Russian, according to his clothes, and he came over to us.

"We got a new worker," he said as he sized me up. "Take care of him, I'm going to the office."

The people stopped in their work and looked at me. The hall was hot, the kapo appeared to be a human being, and the prisoners were Russian POWs. The thought, "It's good here," crossed my mind, "but what do I do in order to stay?" As though in answer to my silent question, the man said, "I am responsible for the work here, my name is Grisha. What did he tell you? What do you know how to do?"

I was quiet for a moment, but decided to trust him. "I do not know how to do anything. I was a student. I told them that I am a blacksmith because I was told that they do not kill blacksmiths... now I do not know what will become of me..."

The man—broad-shouldered, though nearly as depleted and tortured as I was—looked at me quietly, then looked around at the workers grouped around us who had heard what I had said. "You know what happened?" He spread his hands in despair, "we have ourselves a sucker... He doesn't know anything, so he said he was a blacksmith... You know why? He wants to live..." Then he turned back to me, "How old are you?"

"18 years old," I answered quietly. Again he looked at me closely, as though considering my worth. I myself nearly forgot who I was.

"He told me to make lilies, for the garden gate. I do not even know what that is, but I said I would do it."

"Why?" The question was piercing, strange. "Why did you say you would do it? And what were you planning to do, not knowing what it is and you're not even a blacksmith? And what are you?"

"Do you know what they call me and those like me, they call

us 'stuff that comes out of the chimney'..."

I told them briefly what was happening to the Jews. They did not respond, just looked at me. Finally, when my outburst quieted down, the man grabbed a hammer and handed it to me. "Come, learn. We will make a blacksmith out of you by the evening... you will be our apprentice." He smiled, like a man grinning at a good joke, but his eyes did not smile. Nor did I smile. "I will teach you, and in the meantime, the guys will make you some lilies..."

The others nodded their heads in agreement, and after a moment the hustle and bustle of the workshop returned. Everyone went back to their work. A couple of them looked for material to make the lilies. Grisha explained to me that the German meant flowers made from tin and iron, to work them into the bars of the gate as decoration. As he worked, he explained how to hammer out the metal and cut it according to a leaf design. I assisted him to the best of my ability. I knew that I owed him my life. I thought of the many people that I owed my life to and wondered about my fate. Would it last me until the end... and what was to be the end? My hands held the hammer and my eyes were fixed on my savior. I knew that I would never be able to pay him back, just as I would not be able to repay all of the others, and I decided to do my best to please him.

A short while later, the flowers were ready—two pretty iron lilies with tin leaves of a nice size. When the German came in the afternoon to take "the flowers," he found me standing and painting them with black paint, giving them color and shine. He stood puzzling at the sight. "You did this?"

The German kapo was called and approached, and Grisha along with him. "Is it good work?" The officer asked.

"Ja, ja," replied Grisha, nodding his head.

The officer looked at the flowers again and smiled. His look of contempt vanished for a moment. The German could appreciate good work and execution and could not hide it. He pulled a packet of cigarettes from his pocket and handed it to me: "This is for you. Good work..." Before leaving, he said to the kapo, "Take care of this one. He is an excellent craftsman."

I glanced at Grisha and conveyed all my feelings of gratitude. I shared the cigarettes with everyone and a good mood prevailed in the hall.

From that first day of work, I became a blacksmith. From time to time, people would call me, jokingly, "Hey, Lily, come here, bring a board," and I was quick to do what they said. Most of my work was assisting the others, as a kind of apprentice, but eventually I was able to work on my own, even carrying out complex projects.

X.

Twenty-Five Lashes

When I got back to the camp that evening, it seemed like a return to hell. After my time in the smithy, it was much harder to bear the sights of the camp: the multitudes of thin people, near skeletons moving to and fro, the terrible hunger, the despair and the depression all around...

We entered the camp to the sound of the camp orchestra playing, marching to the beat of the drum, as we passed through the lines of SS men. We dispersed among the barracks, and after about a quarter of an hour, at precisely six o'clock, we received our evening meal: a bowl of "soup" and a small slice of bread. We were "free" until seven o'clock to do various things: laundry, mending, haircuts (the maximum length of hair allowed was one centimeter), and checks.

The check was done every evening at the block entrance by the "block elder" and his prisoner-helpers. We were made to undress. If a louse was found on a prisoner, he would be brutally beaten and the one who found it would get an additional helping of soup...

The "block elder" had to choose those prisoners that would be willing to turn in others in exchange for an extra helping. As hunger grew, so did the number of volunteers. After the check, "market" would begin. Frantic negotiations, selling, buying, and exchanging would take place in the toilets, away from the watchful gaze of the guards.

By evening the bathrooms were full. With a feverish excitement, items were exchanged. The goods most in demand were a slice of bread, a piece of potato or onion—anything that would ease the terrible hunger pains. There were arguments as to what was more nutritious—onion or potato? Their value would fluctuate in accordance with the arguments. Many people sold their last shirt and went about in just a jacket with the shirt collar sticking out.

There were people who would do additional work in the barracks—tailors, barbers, and shoemakers—that would get an extra little bit of soup from the "block elder." He wanted things clean and people to look good, whether from some desire to help us or to find favor with the Germans.

The Germans, in their characteristic thoroughness, decided to organize entertainment in the camp—for themselves, of course. An orchestra of prisoners was assembled. Skeletons of people, that in the past had been the great musicians of Europe, played on a stage in the center of the camp for long hours with no rest.

Another form of entertainment was wrestling. Every so often they would choose prisoners for a wrestling "match," surrounded by dozens of armed Germans, shouting and cheering and shooting into the air, or at the "athletes" whose strength failed them or who did not display satisfactory "fighting spirit."

And there was another spectacle for the Germans: "theater." That is how they referred to the hangings that they carried out in the central yard. The "shows" were usually on Saturdays. When we came back from work and stood before the blocks in a large

U-formation, the Germans would hang prisoners gathered for that purpose throughout the day or the week—prisoners that were caught smoking or those that spoke with English POWs, those that were caught stealing or engaging in trade, or for "impertinence to a superior," and, of course, for attempting escape. They referred to these "crimes" as "sabotage"—sabotaging the Nazi war effort. They would leave those hanging to be seen for an extended time. There were instances when the victims would shout at the moment of their hanging, calling for revenge, "Never forget!" and "Tell the whole world!" Eventually the Germans began to stick bandages on the mouths of the condemned before bringing them out to hang. They were not able to shout and the "show" became mute. After the show, the entire formation would pass the hanging. The "block elder" would order that hats be removed, and from there everyone would disperse to their respective barracks.

The entertainment for the Jews was something else entirely. On holidays and sabbaths, there were Jews who would organize hidden prayers. Those that did not pray themselves would listen in silence to the whispering of prayer. On Yom Kippur, our whole block got together and did not eat a thing. Perhaps this was a spark of desire to hang onto the human experience—despite the hunger. One of the guys managed to convince the "block elder" to keep our portion of bread for the following day—and he agreed. We compensated him in various ways all the time, such as smuggling him a cigarette from the factory every so often.

And there were those among us, skeletal though they may have been, who tried to cheer up the general mood and would not let us sink into melancholy. Once in a while, at some quiet moment you might hear singing, stories, jokes, and even plans for the future. One guy who particularly shone in this respect was Abram'leh, a camp veteran who had been there for four whole years.

Many did not make it. There were those who woke up in the morning extremely depressed, and on our return from assembly we saw them hanging on the electric fence, charred. Many were taken out in "selections," the purpose of which was to remove the weak—though it would be more accurate to say that people were selected depending on the mood of the particular German.

The selection always began suddenly. The gong was heard and then shouts of, "Close the barracks, stop!" We were forced to shut ourselves up in the barracks immediately, bolt the doors and windows, and not look outside. When the "block elder" notified us of selections, everyone had to undress. One by one they were brought in to the cell of the "block elder" and we would be given our tickets.

We passed before the eyes of the German soldier, sent from the S.S. headquarters, and he would examine each prisoner closely. When he heard the order, "Go!" the prisoner breathed deeply and returned to his place. If he said to the block elder, "Take his ticket!" it meant, to the gas chambers and then the crematorium. The next morning, during assembly, those without tickets would be gathered, loaded onto a truck, and taken from the camp. The remaining hours of night were unbearable for those condemned to death.

I survived all of the selections. I was young, and I also had the help of my Russian friends at the smithy. But suddenly it appeared that my luck had run out.

At the factory, there were also English prisoners of war. Speaking with them was entirely forbidden, and punishable by death, but as we crossed the factory paths, we would look at one another and even make physical contact. The English looked way better than us. We knew that they were receiving packages from the Red Cross. They were allowed to smoke on the factory grounds. There were good men among them, and they understood our circumstances. A new phenomenon developed: a Brit would light a cigarette, smoke maybe a third or a half of it, put it out, and toss it to the side of the path beside a stone or clod of earth where it was less visible, and would wait until one of us noticed. After some time, when he had left, we would emerge and take the cigarette butt. Some would smoke it in secret, and others would keep it for trading back at the camp. Occasionally they would do this, too, with a piece of chocolate or a small slice of bread. It seems that the English knew that this would save our lives and saw the risk as a way of continuing their own battle against the Germans, which had otherwise ended with their capture.

One day S.S. Officer Raketz caught me smoking. He was the head of the camp's political branch. He called me and asked, "Where do you work?"

"Blacksmith," I answered.

"How is it you have a cigarette?" He asked, sternly.

"I found a small piece," I replied without emotion.

Raketz slapped me hard on the face. I was quiet. He wrote down my number. I wondered why he did not shoot me on the spot with his gun. He left, and I went into the smithy. I said nothing about the incident to anybody.

In assembly that evening, after inspection, the camp commander came on stage and called several numbers, including mine. My friends and brother looked at me in dismay but did not make a sound. While everyone went back to the barracks, five of us remained standing in the large yard. We were sent to the office of the political branch. I was called first. Raketz sat beside a table, beside another S.S. officer. He reviewed the details: "at such and such a time, you committed sabotage—you smoked a cigarette with the intention of causing explosions among the factory facilities!"

"I smoked, but I had no bad intentions," I replied, and again I prayed that he would not kill me on the spot.

"Bring his ticket!" He turned to the kapo that stood at the side. There was quiet. The two S.S. officers observed me with cold eyes. Raketz looked at my ticket. "I see this is your first time, and I will take that into account. You are a blacksmith?"

"Yes," I answered. Would this save me from death a second time?

"The second time you will be hung!" He continued, "This time—25 lashes on the back."

I was taken to the second room. In the center there was a low table, narrow and long, and two big holes on one side. I was ordered to remove my pants. My legs were put through the holes. My hands were tied to the sides of the table with straps. On the wall, across from me, were hanging whips made from leather.

Two kapos approached and ordered me to count the lashes I was getting. I counted with my head down and even saw the drops of blood from my flesh before losing consciousness.

I regained consciousness when a bucket of water was dumped over my head. I was taken out of the brace and released with a push forward, the kapo shouting, "Make yourself run, and fast!"

I fell at the entrance to the barracks and managed to get myself onto my knees—but no more. I thought it was the end of me—and I was relieved. Suddenly I felt hands taking hold of me and raising me up. I looked up and saw before me the redeeming face of my brother Yehezkel, my guardian angel. He stood outside with a friend, Izak, waiting for me to come out, knowing what would happen inside. They lifted me up, draped my arms over their shoulders, and said quickly, "Make it look like you're walking, and quickly, before the kapo comes out!" They dragged me after them towards the barracks. I did my best to move my legs but could not. By the time we got there I had fainted again. They managed to get me inside, place me on a bunk, wet rags, and clean the blood off my body, and for the whole night, cooled my burning flesh, wetting the rags again and again in water they had prepared in their bowls. The following day, they dragged me back to work, this time, unlike usual when I walked with the healthy, but rather on the inside of the formation. I do not know how I managed to pass the inspection at the gate, but I made it to the smithy. I lay down in the corner with my friends on guard. When it came time for inspection, they lifted me and propped me up against a machine. When the supervisor was gone I laid back down.

After a few days, I healed up, although I did not return to my previous state of health. Evidently damage had been done to some internal organs, perhaps the stomach, because since then I have suffered intense pains in my stomach. That was the first and last time I was whipped—and by some miracle, I got off relatively easy. There were those that received fifty, seventy-five, and even one hundred lashes, and were taken from the table directly to the crematorium.

XI.

The Christmas Nightmare

The whipping incident took place about a month before Christmas. As I walked with difficulty, recovering from my wounds, a strange bustle began around the camp. There was much tension in the air, and there were rumors of the Russians advancing. There was talk that something would happen on Christmas. The Germans contributed to the atmosphere of rumors—carpenters brought many planks and metal rods and began to build a large structure that slowly took the shape of an enormous tree. Were the Germans putting up a large fir to celebrate Christmas? There was talk of the Germans' need for propaganda and the photographs that the world would see of holiday celebrations in the camp.

"Commentators" argued that this should be seen as the beginning of the end, signs of German fear of the world's opinion. Far-reaching claims even suggested that the Germans were beginning to prepare for surrender and were arranging evidence in their favor. "This is an order from above to change direction," they said. The installation was enormous: on a base of thick beams they put young trees, covered in leaves. They put large spotlights all around, to light up the tree.

Then came Christmas Eve. There was an assembly of all of the camp's residents. The assembly lot was full with prisoners who had received clean clothes that day. The tree was lit up and dazzling. Even the pessimists were quiet. Lines of armed S.S. soldiers stood all around, shining in their ironed uniforms.

The camp commander rose to the stage beside the tree and began a speech, as usual, about the need for work for the German war effort, of the brilliantly victorious armies and the need to assist them in the work of the home front, and so on. The commander finished his speech and left the stage. In his place rose a different S.S. officer holding a list. He said, "The following numbers must approach the stage immediately," and read out twelve numbers. The kapos, who evidently knew this was what would happen, gathered the men from their different units and brought them to the center. To our surprise we saw that they were from all different nationalities: Jewish, Greek, Gypsy, Polish, French, Dutch, Hungarian, Russian, and German—a political prisoner, according to his marking.

The twelve men were brought before the tree. Suddenly a terrible silence fell over the entire yard and camp—and then the orchestra began to play. Twelve armed S.S. soldiers approached. The kapos, that brought the men, took out twelve nooses hidden among the branches of the tree. Each kapo placed a rope around the neck of his prisoner and the cries of those prisoners mingled with the sounds of the orchestra playing the Nazi anthem. The spotlights lit up the German fir tree—each spotlight directed at the hanging corpse of a prisoner, pulled up to a height of two meters, by some pulley system in the tree.

The anthem ended, and in the fading out of the notes, the groups were marched around the stage and sent back to their barracks. For supper, in light of the holiday, we received two portions of bread instead of the usual one...

But the camp was unusually still. The regular din after a meal did not happen. Everyone was shut up in their barracks. There were barely conversations even inside of the barracks. I saw my bunk-mates lying quietly, terribly crowded together. Then I was overwhelmed by pain. I felt exhausted and my stomach hurt terribly. I left the barracks and walked to the doctor. The doctor had the authority to let patients stay one day at camp. Often even seriously ill patients refused to stay, knowing that a sudden selection would take them to the gas chambers. But staying for one day was not considered dangerous, and I requested the doctor's permission. I no longer cared much about hiding my state.

The doctor looked at my back, checked my stomach, and wrote me a "rest" permit for the following day. With my permit, I received a white cloth label with two red letters on it—I.L., meaning "in Lagger." Any prisoner who stayed at the camp and did not go to outside work wore this label on their back: kitchen and cleaning workers, suspects arrested at the camp on suspicion of sabotage, the sick, and others. I returned to my barracks, collapsed into my bunk, and tried to fall asleep.

The next day everyone went to work. Yehezkel was angry at me for getting a "sick permit," but I must have looked really sick, so he let me be. The camp emptied out. It was a strange feeling to be left behind.

At ten, the gong sounded, and the speakers called anyone who had stayed at the camp to gather immediately in the yard. I left my barracks. Several dozen people entered the yard, all with the white label. Raketz, the supervisor, appeared with a kapo carrying a list. Each person present was asked, in order, the reason for his staying at the camp, and after Raketz gave his opinion, would receive some particular job, according to the list held by the kapo.

I was in a group of ten people that was sent to remove the bodies from the Christmas "fir." I did not even have the strength to be sorry that I had stayed at camp. With the others we walked over to the tree and looked for a way to remove the bodies. The stronger among us climbed the tree and loosened the ropes, and the bodies hit the ground with a thump. We carried them by their arms and legs and set them down beside one another. Afterward, four of us went to get a cart. The bodies were then loaded from the cart onto a truck that took them to the crematorium.

Now we were instructed to take down the tree. We did not know how or where to begin. Despite my pain, I climbed up, sat on a plank covered with branches, and checked the tied ropes. I tried to loosen the end of the rope and in doing so, several branches came free and fell to the ground. At the same moment I heard a shot and felt a strong pain in my leg, which immediately began to spurt blood.

Below stood an S.S. soldier that had come to supervise the job. I was not aware of his presence as I was busy checking the tree. The branches fell beside him and he thought that I had done it on purpose, turned and shot me at close range. "Come down at once, swine!" He shouted angrily.

I sank to the ground, powerless. I waited for the second shot, the release, but it did not come.

"You are lucky today is a holiday!" He shouted. "Otherwise I would kill you on the spot!" The supervising kapo hurried over to us, concerned for his own skin. He kicked me a couple times to satisfy the soldier. The kapo bent towards me and grabbed the collar of my jacket, lifting me off the ground with both hands, and whispered, "Get back to your bunk, but quick! Do not so much as stick your nose outside!" Suddenly I had a flash, as if real, of the previous year's Christmas, and remembered the explosion and my grave injuries, which I suffered from for long months afterward. Some holiday luck...

I pressed my pant leg to my wound to stop the bleeding and limped towards the barracks. I entered the empty block, took off my pants, and saw that the bullet had entered the flesh below the knee, taking out a large chunk of it but, luckily, had not stayed lodged in my leg. I tied a rag to the wound and tightened it well. The "bandage" was immediately sopping with my blood, but the flow slowed to a drip and stopped. I lay there until the evening. There were no medicines, obviously, and the only treatment was to wet the rag from time to time. Yehezkel, furious, fussed around me for a long time.

The next morning, when the bell rang to get up, I stayed lying there. I could not get up in spite of all my efforts. Yehezkel removed the rag and here, the skin around the wound had contracted and turned a strange grayish color, and I was unable to stretch my leg. Yehezkel retied the rag, lifted me on his back, and brought me to the doctor. I do not know how his strength held out, though I did not weigh much by then—but then his weight must have been similar... He left me at the sick hut, took a ticket for the assembly, which one must show if someone is missing, and ran quickly to the yard.

From the doctor's hut I was transferred to the "hospital." For some reason, the Germans took satisfaction in cultivating the hospital and allowed the doctors to run it. Although every so often a truck would come to "cleanse" the hospital of its patients, after a thorough cleansing of the place, new patients would be admitted. The patients lay on a mattress with no sheets, naked, covered with a single blanket. Anyone who dirtied his mattress was severely punished.

The doctor responsible for the hospital, a medical professor before the war, checked my leg. He promptly determined that an operation would be necessary. I was put in a warm bath—an experience I had not been granted in a very long time—but my pain prevented any enjoyment. Another doctor, who served as a nurse, put hot compresses on my wound, to clean it out and remove any dirt. For three days straight they would apply boiling cloth rags to my leg, which made me faint from pain. There were no sedatives to be had. On the fourth day, January 3rd, 1945, at eleven in the morning, I was taken to surgery.

My brother, who came to visit me every evening, knew that during the operation there would be no sedative or anesthesia. He had recruited all our friends together, from the camp and from the factory. They gathered everything they had—cigarette butts, bread, shirts—and traded all of it for a golden crown of a tooth. I do not know who they got it from. They offered the gold to the doctor in exchange for one dose of anesthetic. It took gold for the doctor to consider the risk.

On the operating table, I reminded the doctor of his promise, and he nodded his head. Nevertheless, I saw that his assistants were tying my hands and legs to the table, but then I saw the doctor wet a piece of cotton in ether and hold it to my nose. I inhaled with quick breaths, as deeply as I could before the ether could evaporate, and as I was still struggling to breathe they began to operate. When they stretched out my leg, I cried out and when the knife cut my flesh, the doctor stuffed a rag into my mouth, stifling my screams. I broke out in cold sweat. Several times I lost consciousness until coming back, awakened by the pain.

The doctors cleaned the wound, stitched its edges, covered it with a piece of gauze, and bandaged the leg with absorbent toilet paper; from behind they tied a rod to straighten and stretch the leg. With that, my operation was complete, and I returned to my bed. For fourteen days I did not leave the bed. They changed my bandages, but I did not get any medication. The wound gave off a bad smell and leaked pus. As the days passed, the wound looked worse and caused me constant pain; and all that time I had one eye on the door, anxiously anticipating the truck that would come to evacuate the building...

XII.

The Russians Arrive to Auschwitz

On January 17, at six in the evening, we suddenly heard an unusual sound. An S.S. soldier came into the hospital where I was lying and announced that all patients must immediately report to a medical committee. This stirred up the "hospital" as it was out of the ordinary even for the doctors. As the commotion grew, the head doctor quieted us, saying, "I think that the Germans are evacuating the camp because the front is getting close. Whoever can walk and wants to stay alive must report to the medical committee and give the impression that he is healthy!"

The meaning was plain. Patients in critical condition got up and left. I went out after them dragging my leg, steadying myself on the bedposts along my way.

We passed before the committee—an S.S. doctor and two soldiers. The doctor looked at my leg without removing the bandage. "I don't think this one can walk," he said, sniffing with disgust.

"I can walk," I ventured, "I walked here, and I can walk much more."

"It is a long way to the heart of Germany," he smiled to the soldiers by his sides. "He stays here," he said and he turned to the next patient.

The soldiers pushed me back toward the sick room. I knew that nothing could help me now. I was dragged to my bed in the empty hall. I pulled the worn blanket over my head.

A short while passed but to me it felt like years. Then there was a hand on my shoulder. I turned my head and there was Yehezkel in front of me. "What's up, Mjetek?"

"They won't let me leave. I can't walk." I covered my head again with the blanket. "It's over. It's all over!"

"I am staying with you," Yehezkel said loudly, turning the heads of the other patients in the neighboring beds. "I will stay here as a patient and look after you! We will go together..."

I was silent. To stay with my brother was encouraging, and maybe even a chance to make it out alive. But I said, "No! They are going to kill us. Go. Live. Anyway, I am wounded with this putrid leg. At least you will make it..."

"Doesn't matter. I am not leaving you. We have stayed together this entire time, no?"

The patient lying on the bunk beneath mine rose onto his bony elbows and called to me, waving his hand and fingers. "How are you not ashamed? You want him to stay and die too? It's not enough that we should have to die?! Better that someone will survive to tell our story, all of it! This is criminal! You..." He pointed his shriveled finger at Yehezkel. "You—get out of here! Live! Don't be a fool! You want to help the Germans finish us all? We can die anyway, without you, we don't need your help!" The man burst into heartbreaking tearless wails. His dry, shriveled body would not waste precious liquid and his cries were terrible.

Yehezkel looked at me and stroked my shoulder, then my face. Then he too cried. "I'm staying with you... We have stayed together and we will die together... Like Father and Mother and Miriam..."

We sat together, holding one another silently. We listened to the sounds outside and could tell that the entire camp was preparing to leave. Maybe half an hour passed this way until Izak, my brother's friend, came into the room with our kapo. The kapo approached my brother and said, "Get up! You are coming with us. Good that this one said something, otherwise they would kill you just for this. They would punish me too if you were missing. Come!" Seeing Yehezkel's hesitation, the kapo added, "Those who leave have a much better chance of surviving. What's the point of dying here? You have two minutes to say goodbye!"

Eventually, the two took Yehezkel by the arms and dragged him after them. Yehezkel gave me a final glance from the door, a look of despair and pity, and disappeared. I felt more alone than I had ever been. I lay silent, detached from everything, even my memories, praying for my brother's survival. The noise outside grew. I heard the barking of orders, cries, shots and more orders, and the sound of people marching and getting farther away.

We remained alone in the "hospital," several dozen helpless patients, alone in that large and empty camp. There was still electricity, running water from the taps, and two doctors hovering around us. They were two healthy men who had volunteered to stay with their patients until the end. They gave us food: a slice of bread, a spoonful of jam, and one piece of sausage—where they got it from, we had no idea. Beneath our blankets we were naked, shaking from cold. But the doctors said that there were still Germans in the camp, so it would not be wise to go outside to search for clothes or supplies.

Somebody called for quiet. In the silence that followed we heard the booming of explosions in the distance. There was a burst of excitement and joy: "The Russians! The front is here!" The voices were still far away, and the sounds of the Germans shooting from the camp were close. We knew that they were doing a final killing before the end, and the joy we felt died instantly. We lay tense, waiting...

We waited for three days and the whole time we heard voices, explosions, and shooting within the camp. The Germans exploded and burned the facilities, the barracks, the crematorium, and the gas chambers. One by one they destroyed the damning evidence, and we could do nothing but wait...

In the meanwhile, I made a friend—the patient that had had the outburst during my conversation with my brother. He moved to the bunk beside mine, and throughout our long conversations, we became well acquainted. He was a Russian Jew, from Minsk, named Izak Elkin. He was a partisan, captured in Poland along with others. The Germans did not know he was Russian.

We became very close. Isaac was in better shape than I, but also in critical condition. Every so often he got down from his bed to bring water and to look for food. People would go out to rummage among the destroyed barracks...

On January 20, in the early evening, we heard shouts in our barracks and the voices of soldiers ordering us to get out. They were carrying oil cans and we knew that they intended to burn the place down. Whoever was able to, got up and left. I rose but was unable to move my leg. I looked around in despair. Then Izak came, threw my blanket to the floor and said, "Go to the floor!" I fell onto the blanket, my body stiff with cold. One step after another, he dragged me with him, toward the door and out, into the snow.

They ordered us to organize ourselves into groups of five. We were then put into larger groups of one hundred people per group. They brought prisoners from other barracks as well. To our great surprise, there were about four hundred prisoners remaining at the camp! This time the Germans gave no speech. They were tense and irritable.

Izak and I were in the second group. He turned to me, "I take it that they will kill the first group, and we will have to bury or carry them. I am not doing any more work. I want to be first. I calculated wrong... I do not want to continue..."

"What will you do?" I asked with indifference.

"I'm going to the first group."

"I'm coming with you," I replied.

Isaac advanced and spoke with the two patients standing last among the first group. They agreed to switch. Isaac dragged me to their place. At a distance the sounds of continuous, dull booms could be heard. We were led to a closed corner between three barracks, in a U-shaped formation, and stood. Many fell, wrapped in the blankets, to the snow. The Germans waited. Several of us began to provoke them. For some reason we were possessed. "Shoot already and put an end to all of this!" Someone shouted. "Hitler is kaput!" But the soldiers still did not shoot.

They listened to the approaching explosions and their confusion grew. Then we grasped what the sounds were: planes. Excited shouts were heard, and now the planes were already above us, so close, so impressive. Bombs fell on the camp, clusters of dark spots coming toward us, whistling. We waved towards the planes, even though we knew that the bombs might kill us too. A bomb fell on the third barracks from us and we felt the ground shudder under our feet. Dozens of planes filled the sky. The space was lit up as if in daylight by the illuminating bombs. A truck dashed from the side and with a shrill squeal, gathered up the soldiers that were guarding us. "The Germans are fleeing!" We cried like madmen. We hugged and kissed one another, stunned by the new hope rising up inside us. Izak gripped my shoulder.

"Mjetek! We are alive! We are alive! In spite of everything!"

The shelling continued all night, until morning when the sun came up. The Germans had disappeared. Here and there were heard cries of prisoners who were injured by the shrapnel. People were running between the barracks to avoid the fire, which was being carried by the strong wind. Our group, lying on the snow, was not hurt. We dragged each other to the nearest barracks and arranged ourselves inside.

We entered and found sixty men who, unable to leave, had remained inside. The others had gone out to look for food. They rummaged around the barracks, hoping to find the hiding places of the prisoners who had left.

Those who found anything edible brought it back, like frozen potatoes and dry bread. Izak found a margarine wrapper. We each chewed on it until it became soft enough to swallow. To protect ourselves from the cold we grouped together, three or four to each bunk and covered ourselves with all of our collective blankets. We stayed like that until January 27.

The weak among us died quietly. We no longer had the strength to take the dead out from the barracks. They were just dragged or pushed to the back, farther into the barracks while the living huddled on the other side by the door. Many lingered in the stage just before death, the "Muselmanner" as they were called at the camp.

The hunger was terrible and once, while I was in a kind of stupor, a movement from the foot of the bunk caught my eye. I bent to see a skeletal figure crawling on all fours towards the back part of the barracks, where the dead were. I thought maybe he had hidden food there. I got down and crawled after him, but suddenly I was gripped by horror: he stopped before one of the bodies and bore his teeth into its backside. I pulled at his legs and with my remaining strength, cried, "What are you doing?" He turned to me with an expression crazed with hunger. I slapped him in the face. The man sat on the floor and burst out crying and wailing. When he calmed down, we quietly returned together to our bunk. I climbed up to my bunk and hoped to warm myself by the body of my bunkmate, a withered Hungarian Jew, with whom I spoke from time to time, when we were not staring at the ceiling, powerless. I lay there with my eyes closed. The time passed.

On the sixth day, in the morning, I woke up to Izak pulling at my arm. "Mjetek, get up! Eat!" He handed me a head of white cabbage, entirely frozen, that he had found in his rummaging in the snow. Happily, I shook my Hungarian neighbor. "Wake up, Magyar, there's food!" The man did not move. I shook him. "Get up, you don't understand!" I pushed him in order to awaken him but that light push sent him to the floor, limbs rigid. I screamed and, hearing me, Izak returned. He bent over him, then turned to me. "Don't scream, he died some time ago, maybe yesterday." A chill ran through my body. I had slept beside this man the entire night without noticing he was dead. I was shocked and angry at myself for pushing him off the bunk, but my remaining bunkmates calmed me down. "He wouldn't have been angry with you. Besides, he can't feel anything."

Morale worsened. We were very depressed. We did not understand why the Russians had not arrived. Our hope evaporated. We sunk back into a kind of indifference. Another day passed. We nibbled on snow and were quiet. And then, one early morning, with the sunrise, we heard the rattle of engines. We looked at one another, hesitant, waiting, waiting... Suddenly we heard shouts in Russian. The door opened. At the entrance stood a Russian soldier with a whip in one hand and a rifle in the other.

In Russian he asked, "Comrades, who are you?"

Izak Elkin rose, gripped my shoulder, and shouted, "Mjetek, they came! They are here!"

He shouted this in Russian, out of excitement, and from having just heard the question, rather than in Polish, which we usually spoke to each other. The soldier froze on the spot and looked at us. There were faint chirps from around the various bunks. Izak dragged himself toward the soldier, like a madman. The Russian stared and shouted, "Stop!"

Izak stopped, and in a broken voice, began to explain in Russian, "I am Russian. I was a partisan. Thank you, brothers."

The Russian soldier dropped his gun and burst out crying. He fell to his knees before

Izak. With shaking arms, he scrambled in his pocket, mumbling to himself, words in Russian, among which we could make out, "Jesus, Mary... Jesus, Mary..."

From his pockets he pulled out everything that was there: dry crackers, a little tobacco, a slice of dried pork, and several candies. While he was doing this he kept repeating, "Don't get close to me... don't touch me!" His eyes would dart up at us briefly, full of tears. Our appearance, evidently, was horrible to behold, not of this world, and he could not stand it. Afterward he calmed us in a shaking voice, "Don't worry, comrades... we are just the first to arrive... in an hour or two the army will come and look after you... there are doctors and food... I will send word... we have to move on!"

He left us and we remained, lying there. We were unable to walk. Even the strongest men sat where they were. Afterward, carts arrived. We heard many voices speaking in Russian. The Russian soldiers entered the barracks, handing out food, but the Russian medical officer, stunned by what he saw, ordered them not to give it to us, because in our current state it could kill us...

They gathered us into one barracks, and a group of soldiers was ordered to set up a kitchen. Our cries for food were too much to bear, and the commander instructed them to prepare a soup for us—a soup with real beef, red meat dripping blood. Many of the patients fainted from the sight of the meat. We did not even wait for the soup to cook. The steam began to spread the intoxicating smell of the soup, and we drank it before the meat was even soft. They cut the meat, still dripping, into small pieces and shared them between us. Izak insisted that we not eat a lot. "It's dangerous! We are unaccustomed to it, you can die from it! We will eat more in an hour."

I was too weak to protest, despite my terrible hunger, and I even agreed with the wisdom of his words. Izak left, and when he came back, he was wearing trousers and shoes on his feet. In the meantime, he had gotten me an extra blanket and several crackers.

In the evening, the medical units arrived with an ambulance and medicine. The doctors checked everyone, wrote names, washed and cleaned us and laid us down in the barracks, which had been cleaned, meanwhile, by the soldiers. Each of us, on average, weighed less than forty kilograms, and by the looks on the faces of the doctors, we understood that we looked like monsters. They were afraid to touch us, lest we break in their hands.

Yehezkel, brother

Isser Gerber, soldier in the Polish army, after being discharged

XIII.

At the Hospital in Krakow

The road leading out of Auschwitz and into the outside world was full of vehicles and crowded with people. Drivers slowed, shocked, as they saw us walking along the side of the road. Several stopped in their tracks and turned back to look at us, not believing what they saw. We were creatures from some other world: small heads that were wizened and shaved, darkened slightly by the hair that had begun to grow, and thin and stooped bodies, near-skeletons, peeking out of gaping rags.

I wore a shirt that was cut from a woman's dress and a dirty blanket tied around my waist with a thin rope. My bare feet dragged my body as though some mechanism of bones was operating itself. The shoes that Elkin, my friend and savior, had brought me, along with the rest of the clothes, hung from my shoulder. I was unable to put the shoe onto my swollen and discolored foot, and I figured it would be better to walk barefoot than with only one shoe. At the camp they had tried to convince us not to leave, but to wait.

"Eat, get well. They will fix your leg. You will get clothes from the army. What is so urgent? It's all over, wait."

But we needed to get out. The mind worked on its own, unable to stop, reflect, and consider. It was all urgent. We could not have stayed there so much as another day. We needed to leave, to get beyond those fences, passing gate after open gate out toward the big world. The labyrinth was opened. If we walked long enough we would find our way. We had people to look for. I had to find Yehezkel. We would live. The leg? It would get better on its own.

Passengers in cars took photographs of us. They offered us food and drink, but gently refused, in a whisper, to take us with them, to help us get far away from here. "We are forbidden to give rides," they said. "Strictly forbidden," said the officer in Russian uniform that we encountered one evening. He watched us for a long time as we walked, driving slowly alongside us. Finally he got out of his car and walked with us, stopping beside a Polish house, some distance off the path. He called to us to follow him. We were no longer hungry or thirsty but we were completely exhausted. For the last couple hundred meters I leaned heavily on my friends with my leg dragging behind me, dripping blood and pus and smelling rotten.

The officer brought us into the house, and with a few poignant statements had the whole household surrounding us, waiting on us, but afraid to really look us in the eyes. They served us hot soup and wrapped my leg with a clean cloth. We stayed the night there, and I fell into a death-like sleep, neither thinking nor dreaming.

I awoke to the sound of music. Stunned and confused, I examined my surroundings: a large hospital room, crowded with anxious people all around my bed. I did not know any of them. I looked among them for my friends. I wanted to get up but I was not able. How did I get here? Where was I? My leg was bandaged right up to my stomach.

After the people, having met their first Auschwitz survivor, relaxed, I was told that I was in a hospital in Krakow. I had been brought there by wagon. The people around knew nothing of my friends. They did not see anyone. They would ask around and tell me. It was obvious that they were shocked by my appearance but trying to hide it. I closed my eyes, feeling the mattress beneath me and the sheet on my body, all that softness threatened to drown me. Somebody touched me on the shoulder. I opened my eyes. I did not know him.

"Mjetek, do you remember me?" I shook my head no.

"It's Vitold. I was a friend of Yanek, from the sports association in Warsaw... Remember?"

Yes. Now I remembered. Someone from that previous world. A previous lifetime.

"What are you doing here? How did you recognize me?" I asked, again the Mjetek that he knew.

"I brought you here. I found you on the way... I didn't know it was you but your friend, Elkin, said that he was a Russian citizen, that he had to go to the Russian headquarters to sign up, and that I must take you to the hospital... He told me your name and was frightened because they weren't able to wake you in the morning. You were unconscious for a long time. Don't worry, now you will be well..."

He smiled at me as if to promise. He had a voice of authority, of command. What could I say to him? What a strange coincidence, to meet him here, now. In my head I heard a strange hum, as though someone was slowly scratching into a stone.

"Mjetek, when you are well I will take you with me. I work for the PPR, the Polska Partia Robotnicza, the worker's party. Now we are in power. Now we are the ones deciding what to do. Don't worry. I will come visit you soon..." He smiled again, with his whole face, and left. I lay there silently, like a package being passed from one hand to another and set down, meanwhile, motionless. Don't worry? Worry about what? What was I to think? What to plan? I had to get better quickly and get up. I had to search, to search...

My thoughts were interrupted. Two nurses approached my bed, holding various papers and forms. They were nuns who looked rather severe. They had come to fill out the registration forms that had not been taken care of yet because I had been unconscious.

"Name?" The question caught me unprepared. I could not think clearly. Which name to give...

"Borkovsky. Mjetek Borkovsky," I answered. "Polish... from Warsaw... Political..." I mumbled answers and closed my eyes.

After they left I tried to concentrate, to think about it. Why had I lied? For what? I examined my fear as though I were observing someone else. I did not know what awaited me outside. I had not seen a single Jew since leaving Auschwitz. Were there any Jews left? Would I be given up? If not to the Germans, perhaps to someone else? And I wanted to go and search for my people... Maybe they would not let me go looking for Yehezkel? I decided to stick to my version, that I was Polish, no matter what.

Days passed. I was still in critical condition, exempt from having to participate in morning prayers, which were conducted by the nuns. A short time after the morning prayers, the doctors would come around. One day, they were standing at the edge of my room when suddenly there was a commotion from the end of the hall. Shouts, gestures... at the heels of an agitated nun marched a thin Russian soldier, with a sack on his back and an automatic rifle in his hands. The room was silent. And suddenly, "Mjetek! Finally I found you!"

Elkin, my friend and savior, whom I'd thought I would never see again, was standing before me. The doctor turned to him in

Russian and my friend answered that we were friends, practically brothers because we had been together in the camp and that he had come to say goodbye to me properly before heading to the front. He did not have time to wait until the doctors had finished their rounds; the nurse had not even been willing to listen, which was why he had forced his way in.

We embraced one another. We shed tears of emotion. He told me that when he had been unable to wake me, he got very worried and decided to take me to the hospital. He had taken me to the main road and tried to stop a car, but they all refused to stop. Finally he had stopped an army vehicle, and one of the men in it was Vitold. I already knew the story, but we marveled at the unlikeliness of the chance event. I asked Izak to write to me from the front, to stay in touch. He promised, kissed my forehead, waved to me and left. That was the last time I saw Elkin, my friend and brother. I never heard from him again. I did not even get a single letter. What happened to him I will never know. He was sent to the front and disappeared. I looked for him but found no trace, to this day.

I lay in the hospital in Krakow for about two months. I pretended to be a Polish Christian and made friends with the youngest nurse there. She was from the village and helped the nuns. Once I was better, she began to talk more and more of our shared plans. She invited me to visit her home, her voice warm and her eyes sparkling. One day she brought me a package of clothes, which she had taken from the closet of her younger brother. She followed me closely, as I moved through the phases of recovery, and my limp concerned her so that one morning she brought an expert surgeon with her to one of her morning visits. He checked my leg and explained that although the wound had healed well, the skin had not mended properly. There was a large furrow and if I did not want to continue limping, I would need another operation...

I did not want another surgery, which would mean further prolonging my stay in the hospital. I believed that the leg would sort itself out, as my drive to get out of the hospital grew from one day to the next. I was also afraid of the growing friendship with the young nurse, who did not know who I really was. I decided that I had to get out of there as soon as possible. After a sleepless night, I got up with the first light of morning, put on the clothes that were in my small cupboard and put the few documents in my possession into my shirt pocket: the release form from Auschwitz, signed by the Russians, and the hospital registration form. Then I quietly left the hospital. Nobody stopped me nor asked me where I was headed. I went into the street to look for the train station.

Train rides for survivors of the death camps were free. I showed my document and for the first time, something good came of my terrible past. The free pass was intended to make it easier for survivors to get back home and seek out their relatives. At the train station were hanging many lists of names of people seeking their loved ones.

I eagerly read all the lists, my heart beating faster and faster. Finally, I took a seat on a train car, gripped with sadness and despair. I had not seen a single name I knew on all those lists. I did not even have anything to write my own name with. I also had no address to give. I set off on a long journey with no end in sight: the journey of searching.

XIV.

Smugglers

By the time I got to Lodz it was evening. I was tired and hungry. I had no relatives in this city, but there were notices... I looked and looked. Clear handwriting and messy handwriting. Yiddish, Polish, Russian, and even German. I saw nothing of those I was looking for. I wandered around the streets. People came and asked me questions. I was among Jews.

I was directed to a special office established in the offices of the new Jewish community in Lodz. I waited for the secretary, but he was busy with preparations for the party celebrating the city's liberation and instructed me to come the following day. I went up to the fourth floor, curled up in a corner, and fell asleep. Below there were Jews singing and dancing. In the morning I returned and sat to wait for the secretary just outside his office. When he arrived he made no mention of my appearance, my wrinkled clothes, my unshaven face. After a short conversation, I received a ticket for the community kitchen: half a kilogram of bread and one hundred grams of fried fat...

I dragged my legs, limping, to the community kitchen. There was a line of maybe a hundred men and women. Eventually I reached the window. The Jew handing out the food reached his hand out to me, "55 groszy for the food!" Then, hearing I had no money, "Get out of the window. Get money and come back."

"I have approval from the secretary," I implored.

"So go to the secretary and get money from him. Get out of here or you'll get a smack in the face!" He said sharply, sticking his hand out at the woman standing behind me.

The woman glared at him and turned to me, "Give me the ticket. I will get it for you!" I was powerless to protest. She made good on her promise, handing me the bread and fat after paying the necessary amount, mumbling several words as she did so. I thanked her. She looked at me with a mixed expression, shrugged her shoulders and walked off.

I walked around the streets. My legs carried me to the train station. My eyes were filled with tears and I did not see what was around me. I bumped into someone. The man cursed and pushed me toward a bench. I sat, tears streaming silently down my face. The sensation of tears slowly rolling down my cheeks was strange, and I felt like someone else was crying, not me. The man I had bumped into sat down beside me. He waited for me to calm down then bombarded me with questions, which I answered briefly. Again I felt completely indifferent.

"I did not find anybody. I have nowhere to go. I have no money. I don't know what to do."

The man sat there quietly for a while. Then he said, "Would you like to come with me?"

"Where?"

"I am going to Danzig. You can search there, maybe you will find someone. We'll go, we'll earn money, and you can go home and look for your relatives."

"Ok," I replied.

"Listen, give me your release papers so that they will let me on the train. You show them the number on your arm and say that you lost your documents. Ok? I will help you. I have lots of money." To prove his words, he pulled a piece of smoked meat from his pocket. "Take this, eat." I ate. I agreed. The main thing was that I would have someone to talk to. The main thing was that I was not alone.

We passed the inspection and boarded the train without difficulty. In the car we squeezed onto there were six seats and only two passengers. One was very young, a girl of maybe 17, and the other girl was several years older. The train left the station and we began talking to one another. The younger girl turned to me, "You are traveling to Danzig to search?"

"Yes," I replied, thinking she meant searching for relatives, but what she said next clarified my misunderstanding.

"You shouldn't bother. There's nothing there anymore. We are going farther, almost to Berlin. There they have lots of things that they gathered. It's worth checking."

I did not understand what she was talking about, but my travel companion's expression showed that he understood very well. They began a lively conversation, recalling prices, considering the values of different items and the demand for them—a real business talk. My new friend turned to me, "Want to join? Together we will be four, we can get almost anywhere, especially with your papers. The Germans left a lot of valuable things that they collected from others and now it is left ownerless. Whenever there is chaos there are things to take and money to be made... to the city merchants, the black market—everything can be sold!"

"But that is stealing! What if they catch you?"

"It is not forbidden. Who's asking? Everyone is doing it. Listen, don't be afraid. Come with us and be a mensch. What do you have left in your life now anyway?"

That was a good question and I had to give it some thought. I felt like a marionette, being manipulated. Suddenly it hit me that up until now, since the Germans had come, I had not been independent. I was always with someone else, helped by someone, guided, waiting for suggestions, for protection. What was I to do now? I still was not completely well. I had nothing. And really, what did I have in my life?

"I'm coming with you," I said. "But I can leave whenever I want, ok?"

"Ok!"

They breathed deeply, and continued to chatter and joke, remembering more names of places and prices. I quietly listened to their conversation and became one of them, the "makhers." There were German treasures that, in their words, had been plundered from the Jews and others. We became a group. The two young Polish girls were sisters: the elder, Halina, whose husband had been killed in the war, and her younger sister Marisha. The young man introduced himself as Boris. We did not ask one another for family names. Halina turned out to be the most energetic among us and became our leader.

We got to the Deutsch Krone station. From there we continued on an army train headed for Frankfurt. We waited for a whole night at the station and not a single other train came. Day and night we traveled with Russian soldiers until arriving at the outskirts of Frankfurt, East of Oder. We leaped off the train while it was moving slowly and entered the city, somewhat scratched up. It was a ghost town, an empty neighborhood, dark and quiet. We wandered the streets, trying not to make noise. Eventually we found a house whose door opened easily. We entered the ground floor. Even in the dark we were able to see that the house was furnished and orderly, as though its inhabitants were quietly asleep in the next room. But there was not a soul to be found and so we spent the night.

Our rest was soon disturbed by a Russian patrol that was passing through the street and must have heard our voices. Again, my Auschwitz release form worked wonders, just like on the train: they looked at me strangely for a long while, rolled my name around in their mouths, and asked us to come with them to the headquarters to register. Halina jumped to her feet mischievously. "Why don't I come with you and you let them sleep, they are so tired from the journey," she reasoned. Two soldiers went with Halina and the third stayed with us, his eyes following Marisha with interest. When Halina returned a short while later she was playful and happy. She had brought with her cigarettes, matches, candles, and sausage.

"There is a party at the headquarters and I am invited. You stay here and sleep, they won't cause you any trouble. This soldier will look after you," she said, indicating the soldier that had stayed with us. Before she left she turned to me and whispered, "Keep an eye on Marisha with him around, so that nothing happens to her, got it?" She glanced worriedly at the soldier and left. The soldier spent the entire night ceaselessly attempting to woo Marisha. We protected her in a special way: with jokes, with threats disguised as jest, and through arranging ourselves so that she went to sleep between the two of us, preventing the soldier from getting too close to her. We did not close our eyes the whole night. In the morning, Halina turned up with a document permitting us to roam about undisturbed. Having heard what we had to say, she scolded the soldier and sent him back to the headquarters as though she were his direct superior.

When she looked at me, Halina's eyes sparkled. She hugged her sister and said, "He's good for you, Marisha, right? He looked after you? He's a good guy!" I panicked. I knew that tone, similar to that of the nurse at the hospital. I had no intention of getting together with Marisha, and I knew that my days among this group were numbered.

Evidently, Halina had managed to get more than just the transit document from the headquarters. Her services must have been very generous, as she had been lent a carriage and two horses for one week, to load whatever treasure we found and bring it to the train station.

Over the course of that week, we gathered anything and everything of value. We did not find jewelry, money, or small valuables—we had been preceded by soldiers. But we took furniture, tools, curtain fabrics, and more. We brought it all to the house where we had stayed that first night, and our pile grew and grew. After a week, in which Halina had spent her days gathering valuables and her nights at the headquarters, we got back on the road to return to Poland.

To this day I do not know how or to whom she managed to sell the treasures we amassed. But one day I found myself in Halina's house, with Marisha sitting at my side, looking at me with admiration, when Halina shoved a wad of banknotes into my hand—my portion of the loot.

One hundred and fifteen thousand zloty! That was serious capital. I stared at the money, not believing my eyes, and heard Halina say, "Brother-in-law, you are rich! Now we can make you man of the house!"

Until now, Halina had not spoken so plainly. Her words hinted that if I were not to cooperate, I might not receive my share of the money. I chuckled bitterly. I was not really considering marrying Marisha, of course. And so then what, to give up that money and leave? How? With that money I could finally be independent. I smiled at the sisters. We drank vodka as though closing a deal. I hid the money in my coat.

"Sure," I said, "We'll have a wedding after I return. I want to go to Warsaw to see what happened with my family. If everything is ok, I will bring them to the wedding too!"

I hugged Marisha and felt sorry for her. I knew that I would not see her again, but there did not seem to be another way out.

XV.

Joining the Security Service

Back on the train. Alone. Mjetek Borkovsky the Pole, Mjetek Bomberg the Jew, searching for his family, desperately looking and finding no one. Slowly the thought crept in: there is nobody to find. Nobody is left and there will be no more. Only you remain, only you exist. And the train moves on...

We got to Skarzysko. I have to wait the whole night for the train to set off for Warsaw. I went into the station canteen, ordered a beer, and sat down. The time passed. Suddenly a group of security people in army uniforms appeared. They checked IDs, carrying lists of wanted people: workers' underground members against the government or wandering refugees.

At night it was easier to find the homeless, the identification-less, who were forbidden to be in the streets at the train station. The soldiers got to me. The one speaking was an officer in Polish army uniform. He spoke to me politely.

"Excuse me, I must ask for your identification. I am with the Security Service."

I handed him my ID. I stared at the commander. I thought I was dreaming. This could not be. Things like this don't happen. Another dramatic meeting?

"Yanek?" I asked hesitantly. The officer's mouth dropped

open. "Mjetek? Mjetek Bomberg? You're alive?"

Those sitting in the small canteen, crowded and smelly, stared at us curiously. Yanek pulled me after him to a side office. Yanek, my friend, Yanoush, we had called him, from that period before everything, when I was a promising athlete and was respected for my physical abilities. Yanek the Pole from Warsaw, who knew my brother, my friends, my childhood. Together we had posted notices decrying the Germans and sang underground songs.

I told him the short version of my story. My doings, my searching. I remembered Vitold and his help and Yanek smiled: "Yes, Vitold is a good guy. Maybe we will meet again."

About himself, he told that he had joined the partisans and lived in the forests. When the Russians came, he was transferred along with many of his fighting friends to the Security Service, took special courses, and reached the rank of captain. Then at last he said,

"Mjetek, I have a suggestion for you. Do you want a chance to get revenge on Germany? I am willing to give you a chance. Come work with us; you will have free reign, practically, to do what you like. You will wear our uniform and you can do what you want. We are catching them and those that cooperated with them. We have already punished a great many ourselves..."

Suddenly an exciting image came into my mind: me, dressed in uniform, armed, approaching an ex-S.S. officer, standing at attention before me, and hitting him over and over. I was shaken from that dream. I waited a little. The scene seemed imaginary.

"I'm ready," I said.

As a Polish Security Service person I would be in a position of authority, of power. Maybe it would help me in my search and in rebuilding my life.

The enthusiastic Yanek wasted no time, and the next day I

was already introduced to the Security Service human resources manager at Skarzysko. Yanek immediately informed him that I was Jewish, although we had decided to keep my Polish name Borkovsky. The man, also with the rank of captain, agreed to take me on a trial basis, on condition that another person serve as a guarantor for me. They required two recommendations from party members, ideally public figures that could be trusted. I was also asked to write a brief "life/personal history." I did that there on the spot, recalling just facts without details. Yanek went out to find me another reference and indeed found one. The fact of my being Jewish worked to my advantage—thanks to anti-Semitism, I could not be suspected of favoring the Poles or the Germans, and I had never been a fascist, only a victim. Surely the desire for vengeance would make me a good and loyal soldier... I did not argue with that. I would rise to the challenge, even with some of my thoughts locked away.

I was accepted. They arranged the papers I needed, including an ID card. And so began my time in the Security Service. I got to know the building. The security measures taken there were extremely rigorous. It had three floors and housed the most important offices. Fifty meters from there was an additional, smaller building, in which transit papers were given out, and "passes," permits to enter the security services building. There were guards in every corner that thoroughly checked anyone entering or passing. After detailed description and training, I was assigned to be a guard at the entrance. I was provided with a uniform, gun, and papers. My job was easy: I had to stop anyone who wished to enter, check their identification, and tell him which office to go to. I had to call the office to ensure that they were ready to receive him. If the answer was positive, I would take his ID and give him a pass, on which I wrote the critical details of his identity. On another form I wrote the precise time of entry and, when he left, of exit. In order to get permission to leave he had to bring approval from the office he had visited, where it would be noted at what time he had finished with his business there, in order to prevent him wandering around the building freely. If everything was in order, he would get his ID back and leave.

I worked as a guard for six weeks. I met all kinds of people. I listened, asked, and learned quickly. The salary was good, and I had few expenses. I did not want for money. I used it only to buy clothes and a couple essentials.

The staff at the office was enthusiastic and proud of themselves. They were very loyal and saw their work as more than just a source of income. In the evening there were meetings, lectures, and ideological arguments intended to strengthen the loyalty and appreciation of the privilege of working "for the homeland and the people." I got to know the employees in the different departments and their roles: the department of espionage, counterespionage, the lab for fingerprinting, quartermaster, vehicles, and others. When I learned everything that I could learn, I approached the station commander, Major Kazhimirsky, and requested a transfer to a more substantial position—to the investigation department.

"There," I explained to my commanding officer, "there is direct contact with Germans and anti-Semites, with Poles that cooperated with the Germans and enemies of the regime and others. I want to do important work," and I concluded, "and I believe I will!"

I returned to work full of worries and hopes, after being promised that my request would be discussed. Several days later, I was called to the office and informed that my request was approved and that I would be sent to a training course for investigative officers. "The course will last three months. If you do well in it, you will be an officer and you can do work that is truly important."

I could not stand still. I thanked my commanding officer and returned his strong handshake. The address on the invitation to the course was in Kielce, a large regional city between Skarzysko and Warsaw. About fifty young, excited men gathered at the place, many former partisans and members of the underground. Only afterward did I realize that I was the only Jew among them. We were ushered into a cafeteria and given breakfast, then awaited instructions. They came from the mouth of the hardened major, and all of us got onto trucks covered with tarps. We traveled for a long time, and not a single man touched the tarp or tried to peak out, wary of the eyes of others.

When the trucks stopped, we found ourselves in a magnificent estate in the heart of the forest, which had been confiscated from the nobility and allocated to the Security Service authority. The place looked like a fairyland: big fields, groves, and flowering gardens. The interior was also impressive: dining room, kitchen, spacious bedrooms, comfortable beds, a drawing room in which there was a player piano, and more. The course commander, the same one that had collected us in Kielce, explained that the course would last, as said, for three months and at its end there would be tests. Whoever passed would be given a suitable position. During this time we would be entirely confined to the grounds of the estate. There would be no time off and no visitors. Letters out would be subject to rigid censorship and it was forbidden to tell anyone where we were.

"And you should know," concluded the course commander, "that at the end of the course, the location will be changed, and the next course will be carried out in a different place such that should anyone babble after the course it will not cause any damage, and in any case I advise you not to babble!"

Nodding and whispering were heard all around. The men considered this. For me there was not much to consider: House? Family? Letters? The few friends I had made in Skarzysko, or my friend Yanek, knew that I had gone to the course, and anyway were not expecting letters. Nobody got up or asked to leave. The course began.

We spent three months at the estate. The daily schedule was routine: morning exercises at six, breakfast, and organizing the rooms. From eight to one—lectures with short breaks between until lunch. Two hours of rest, and afterward, practical studies, training, and drills, usually until ten at night. Sometimes there were nighttime activities. The lecture topics were varied, suited to the needs of the role: foreign policy, domestic policy, objectives and functions of government, economics, psychology, social behavior, and primarily—methods of interrogating: how to get the best results. A considerable portion of the classes was dedicated to getting to know different weapons, how they worked, how to use them and look after them, and of course—shooting practice as much as possible. We also learned how to use explosives, how to take apart mines and traps; we learned to navigate in the field in the dark and do surprise searches. The lecturers and teachers were Polish and Russian. They were introduced to us only using their nicknames.

About a month after the start of the course, something happened that was to alter the course of my new life. The guys there knew I was Jewish. I was proud of myself. The studies were not hard and I tracked my own progress with interest. I felt that my body was getting stronger, my muscles were working well, and my self-confidence grew. Some guys there became friends but others became estranged. One particular group of young men stood out, who were always together as a gang. They ignored my existence, would not greet me, and whispered when I excelled at some demonstration. One day we were sitting in the garden, waiting for a lecturer, stretched out on the shady lawn. Suddenly, a small stone flew at me, and then another. I realized that this was a deliberate provocation and I sat up. Another stone hit me, and the thrower did not even attempt to hide himself. I turned to him and said, "I request that you stop. This is childish. It is unsuitable for a man who wishes to become an officer!"

He grinned and threw another stone at me, while his friends laughed. I got up, approached him, and without a word, slapped his face with all my strength. Mayhem ensued. Several fell on me and others came to separate us before a fight developed. They held me and him and our warring continued verbally. The instructors showed up and settled the matter. I requested to see the course commander who received me with a grave expression. I knew I had to say what I felt, even if it might jeopardize my continued participation. I tried to speak quietly.

"I cannot continue the course, Commander. I feel good here, I am learning the materials, and I enjoy the studies. But there is antisemitism here. I will have no business with anti-Semites. I have had a large enough dose of that already."

The commander stared at me and his eyes softened. "I will deal with it," he said, "return to the lecture!"

During the afternoon break, we were called to gather in the cafeteria, earlier than usual. The course commander entered, and in the quiet of his entrance, spoke directly, "Whoever threw the stone that began the fight earlier—get up!"

Nobody stood. A buzz of protest filled the room. Voices were heard in favor of and against. Suddenly the culprit stood and said, "I got him back, sir, because he threatened me with a gun!"

The guys cried out, "That's not true! He's lying!"

Several shouted, "It's true, it's true!"

I observed the scene playing out before my eyes and in a flash I knew that I had not seen the last of this issue. Germans, Poles—the hatred was there, whispering secretly and arising out of dark corners. I will not be able to fix it, but this time I was determined to resist and to defend myself.

The commander waited for quiet and continued in a low, moderate voice, "I am ashamed. This young man has suffered so much in his life until now. He was in the underground, then in a living hell, with the constant danger of death. If you are still able to hate him—I am ashamed of you. He will stay here—he will be very advantageous to the homeland."

There was a deep silence. Then he spoke, and his words fell like thunder, "You!" The commander pointed at the anti-Semite. "You are going home. The course is over for you. Go to the office and take your papers!"

I did not utter a word. Out of nowhere, the image of Yehezkel arose before my eyes, his friend dragging him away from me, arguing that there was still a chance to live and that I was lost anyway.

"I am still alive, brother. There are people who still care, and with those people in the world, there is still reason to live!"

The exams at the end of the course were thorough, testing our knowledge of every area we had studied: use of documents, putting together an investigation file for the court, judgment, authority of the investigator, operating a weapon—nothing was neglected. We never saw the grades, but evidently we all passed the course successfully. Now we were officers. That evening there was a wild end-of-course party. There was much drinking, high spirits, and the crowning glory: dozens of young women brought from the city to dance the boys around with cheer and enthusiasm.

XVI.

Life as an Investigating Officer

We returned to Kielce. There, in the building where we had gathered before setting off for the course, the files had already been prepared, laying out the roles and locations to which we were placed. I opened my file and saw that I was to stay in Kielce and work in that region.

I was directed to the four-story building, which in the past had been used by the Gestapo and now served as the main base of Kielce's Security Service. I entered the building with mixed feelings and thought to myself, "You are a new man, Mjetek. You are on the other side of the barricade. If only my parents could see me..." I cleared the thoughts from my mind. I went to Intelligence and presented myself in a clear and steady voice. The job had begun.

There were eight investigators working in the investigation department, and I was one of them. Each investigator had a room as an office and for conducting interrogations with a soldier guarding the door. There was a buzzer on the table connected to the corridor where there were additional guards. The guards, which also served as prison guards, took instructions from us. The basement of the building was used as a jail. There were ten cells, each of which could hold up to twenty prisoners. The process of bringing a prisoner for investigation was fixed and well defined. The investigator would fill out a document of invitation for questioning, directed to the prison officer. The guard would bring the form to the officer, who would sign the form letting the detainee out for questioning and *take* him into his custody. Upon his return, the guard would receive a return form, which he would then transfer to the investigator's files.

During the interrogation, the prisoner was suspect but innocent until proven guilty. If it turned out throughout the investigation that the man was innocent, the investigator recommended that he be released. After filling out the necessary forms, the man was released and sent home. If there was evidence of his guilt or if he admitted to it, a detailed indictment would be written up, passed on to the prosecutor, and presented to the court. It was against the law to use force for interrogating, beating, or torture, but the law was not always followed. It turned out that the simple and ignorant among the prisoners needed a few blows in order to open up, as if the shouting and beatings freed them from responsibility or having to stay quiet. Others were approached gently, speaking with a silver tongue. We listed all the possible methods: convincing, temptation, confusion and reprimand, as well as a prolonged perseverance that worked on the nervous system. One tactic seemed particularly successful: questioning on the day of execution. I did not like this approach. There were too many memories related to it. But one time I felt the need to use it.

I was investigating two farmers, guilty of possessing unlicensed weapons. The offense was severe, since they had not reported the weapon to the police and were not even able to explain how the weapon had come into their possession. "We found it in the fields," was the answer to all of my questioning. I observed their small, squinting eyes, and the smiles of hate within them.

Their interrogation had already lasted for two days and in this time, my resentment of them grew, a deep, inexplicable and irrational resentment. I decided to implement the last trick. I rose from my seat, hit the table angrily, and shouted, "I have had enough of you! I do not care if you do not tell the truth, either way you will go to the same place!"

I let several minutes pass, while I wrote a single line on the investigation file, adding an elaborate signature. I pressed the buzzer and the guard entered. "Take them back to the cell!" I ordered. "I am finished with them."

They left and returned to their cell. I called a second guard in and explained to him what I wanted. He nodded, smiling, and headed to the basement. The two suspects had not had the chance to sit down when the second guard entered with the prison chief, telling them, "You have ten minutes to pray..."

Their tone became quiet and serious. The guard came out to the corridor and indicated with his finger that everything was fine. Ten nerve-wracking minutes passed, and the scene changed again, but this time only one of the prisoners was ordered to get up. With shaking arms and legs the man left his cell, followed closely by the nervous gaze of his friend. Afterward, shots were heard and the guard returned alone to the cell.

"Now it is your turn," he said to the second prisoner, and made a gesture across his throat. They went out the corridor, the man barely able to stand. I waited for him in the corner. "Maybe now you would like to talk? This is your last opportunity!"

"I got the rifle from my friend!" he shouted suddenly.

Back in the interrogation room he told the entire story of how and when he had gotten the rifle. According to him, his friend would catch partisans that had come to find food. They then robbed them of their weapons and belongings before handing them over to the Germans. As his story unfolded, he sat up straighter, like a man certain that now that he had said his piece he would be safe. I pressed the buzzer and the guard brought in the second farmer. They stood, mouths gaping, looking at one another, and now the true story flowed out of them. Indeed, the second farmer's story was not so different from the first, except that the two had worked together as one. The search of their house turned up items plundered from partisans and Jews, a great bounty that they had acquired by blood.

Another incident, which incorporated nearly all the elements of drama, disturbed us for a long time. The heroine of the story was Berta, a Polish girl, accused of collaborating with the Nazis, handing over people of the underground resistance, and naming names of "the enemies of the Reich" for the sake of her own self-pride. Her file was given to me, but I only worked on it for two days, without a lot of results, until I became sick with festering wounds, which spread over my arms and legs and I had to take time off. I transferred her file over to another investigator, went on leave, and entirely forgot about the matter of Berta.

One Saturday, about two months later, I was the officer on duty in the building. The long work hours were over, and the building was quiet after most of the employees had left. I prepared for the extended hours of duty, polished my shoes to save myself the trouble the following morning, and dealt with various matters. Suddenly the phone rang, and the agitated voice of the prison officer came on: "Berta is shouting and going crazy. She won't quiet down. Come see what's going on."

I went down to the jail. "I don't feel good," shrieked Berta at my questioning face in the cell window. "I want a doctor! I am sick! Bring me a doctor!"

I called the office doctor, who quickly appeared and entered the cell along with the prison officer on duty. When they came out, he said in a strange voice, "Call the commander, urgently!" To my questions he responded, "I cannot tell you anything. I will only speak with him." The commander answered my call quickly and the two of them shut themselves in his office and I resumed my work, curious but not disturbed.

The following day, on Sunday morning, all of the security officers were called to report to the commander. He stood before us, and his speech shocked us. "I request that the officer who raped Berta identify himself!"

His words hit us like thunder on a clear day. Just like that, without preparation or questions. Nobody moved. I felt as though the blood were leaving my head. Berta was brought to the office, and with a swift movement, as though performing a role on stage, pointed at the officer to whom I had transferred her investigation file when I fell ill. According to Berta, he had promised her good treatment if she had cooperated willingly, but she had firmly refused, and yesterday he fell on her and raped her. There were no witnesses aside from the fact that the guards had been told not to come in until called, even if they heard shouting. The doctor confirmed the truth of her statement, after performing an examination.

Our friend denied guilt entirely. His face was gray, and his lips trembled, "It's not true! She is lying, it isn't true!" The commander was overcome with fury and did not listen to him. "You are banned!" he screamed. "I will present two claims against you: rape and disgracing the uniform! You will not be an officer if you are capable of doing something like this!" His voice was hoarse, as if to relieve him of the pain of his disappointment in the man.

All of us went away to our offices, stunned, without a word. We were in bad spirits and did not deal well with the prisoners that day or the day following. Our friend sat in jail and waited for his trial.

Three weeks passed. The day was relatively quiet, and I was able to relax in my armchair and read a book that had interested me for some time. I was interrupted from my reading by the sound of heavy, irregular steps. The door opened and in walked a soldier from the guards' division, completely drunk. He spoke without pause, his words confused and his voice changing, screaming and hoarse.

"I have to talk to you," he said, though I could barely understand his jumbled speech. "Something very important, you will laugh, see how smart my friend is," he stammered, adding a juicy curse, and continued.

I did not understand what he was saying so I made like I was not interested. I had learned that people prefer to open up to someone who responds with indifference, as though they do not care to hear.

"There are those who know how to live," he whined, "and there are always those who pay the price for them..." He cursed, then said, "Here my friend was living the good life, and nothing happened to him...." The man yawned and looked as though any second he might crash to the floor and fall asleep.

"How great a life can you live here," I asked indifferently, carefully. "Don't tell me about life in our line of work..." I left the sentence open, dismissive, and he shook his head angrily, "You don't know anything... he slept with a beautiful woman, and someone else is lying in the basement in his place..." he broke into a laugh, let out a number of curses and burst into drunken crying.

I became alert, as though electricity was running through me. I hoped he had not noticed, and I asked him, "What's the problem with sleeping with a woman? You don't have to be smart for that. Who can't? You're just messing with the brain..." I waved my hand in front of his face, as a provocation.

His crying stopped. "Yes, anybody can. But not in this building, my dear..." He tapped my shoulder angrily. "And Kowalski did it here. Really, with our prisoner, a good piece! You really know something, you..." He turned and spat, disgusted.

I gently sat him down on the armchair I had vacated. I felt that my eyes had grown inside my face, as though they could not bear the weight of this new information. The man rested his head against the chair and let out a snoring sound. Quietly, I left the room, locking the door behind me. I used the telephone in the corridor and carefully dialed the commander's number.

"Urgent situation!" I answered him. "Get over here as fast as you can." When he came, I eagerly told him the story. His shoulders rose and he stood up straighter. He felt, it seemed, like me. He immediately sent orders, the investigating officers were called to report and a group of soldiers went out to look for the soldier Kowalski.

The activity in the office lasted into the night. The drunk soldier had woken up and, realizing that he had already spoken, retold the story freely. Thanks to his testimony, Kowalski's also ceased to deny it. Berta was also brought to interrogation—and by morning the entire matter had been exposed, cleared up, written, and signed.

Evidently, after three months of investigation, Berta understood that the indictment against her was nearing its end, and soon she would have to appear in court. She, who had brought death to dozens of people, knew that her sentence would be death, and decided to do something that would shake up the building and require a new investigation. In this way she hoped to postpone her trial and gain more time. One of the nights, after her interrogation was over, she returned to her basement cell with the soldier escort. On the way she asked for permission to enter the soldiers' toilets. This was forbidden, of course, but when she begged flirtatiously, the solder agreed, on the condition that the door remained open. She entered, and after several seconds called him in after her. When he entered, he found her naked, her arms spread seductively. The man had no experience, as she had suspected beforehand. She returned to her cell, waited a little, and then began shouting. When the doctor came, she accused the investigating officer of rape. The doctor confirmed that indeed violent sexual intercourse had occurred not long before.

Our friend was released and our commander sincerely apologized to him in front of all of us, giving him extra days off. The soldier got the punishment that he deserved and Berta was put to death by hanging two months after the incident, as decided by the court. However, since then it was decided that no officer should conduct an investigation alone but would be assigned a clerk who would record the process of the investigation in the protocol.

XVII.

Involvement in the Kielce Incident

Work was conducted, for the most part, routinely. For a time, it did not require all of my resources of will and ability in order to manage the various assignments, and my hours outside of work were freed up to continue searching. I did not request any special days off for this purpose. In all the places I got to—villages, towns, and cities—I always set aside time to visit the offices of the committees or municipalities as well as heads of the Jewish communities, if there were any in that place. I carefully examined each list, and in each new place added my own name, the details of my family, and my current address. I sent letters to any organization I heard of that concerned itself with reuniting relatives. I visited Ostrowiec. Many times I visited Warsaw, walked through the ruins, around the horrific evidence of what had been, and searched for familiar places.

My Polish friends were also aware of my search, and would often report to me the responses to their questions regarding the fate of the Jews from Ostrowiec and Warsaw. We searched for survivors from the convoys evacuated from Auschwitz to Germany when the Russians approached; I repeated the name and description of my brother countless times; I looked for his friends or anyone who knew of their fate; I searched for Isser and

Izak—but all of my searching was in vain.

I met Poles I had known, but not one of my Jewish acquaintances. I heard miraculous stories of survivors that made it, but not one of my people had survived. I refused to give up hope, as long as my brother Yehezkel was among the living. He had been healthy and went in order to be saved, in order to live. Where was he? I dispatched letters and requests to Germany itself. I sent messages to be broadcast on the radio. But not one person made contact... they did not know, had not heard, there were no witnesses to the fate of those Jews who had marched into Germany. It was as though there was a total break between me and my past. It was as though someone had taken an enormous eraser and erased everything completely.

It seemed to me that from now on my life would continue in the same way: work, no family, a few friends, meetings with groups of Jews in the city and outside of it, and more work. For a long time I wondered over and over to myself how it was that a man would not feel in advance that his life is about to change suddenly and completely, though nothing could adequately prepare him or warn him.

I was sent to participate as an observer at a convention of foreign journalists. My job included constant listening to check that there were no "subversive elements" among the participants. I had a certificate as a "journalistic observer," and I was also invited to a party that was being thrown for the journalists, at the Bristol hotel in town. I wore evening attire but did not neglect to bring my small gun, which I carried with me at all times. The party ended at three in the morning, and I stayed the night at the hotel. Although we did not fully admit it, walking through the streets at night was very dangerous, due to the large number of robberies as well as murders and assaults on security personnel, soldiers of the regime and even Jews. In the morning, I set off on my route towards the office. I ran into an acquaintance, a Polish lawyer who, to my consternation, continued on simply saying to me, "Be careful!"

I walked on slowly, hesitant. What had happened? I saw people running in the street. Voices were heard in the distance. I was overcome by a heavy, oppressive feeling. In the shadows of the entrance to a nearby house, I took out my gun, cocked it, and returned it to my coat pocket.

I followed the crowd and, as I had feared, came into Pallanti Street, a little dead-end street, where there was already a crowd of loud, nervous people. In this street, at house number seven, were the offices of the Jewish community. At that time, a group of about eighty young men and women were staying there, as a sort of "kibbutz," in preparation for their hoped-for aliyah to Palestine.

As a Jew belonging to the security services, I often brought members of the community letters and money from the central community in Warsaw. I had visited the "kibbutz" many times, spending time with its members, conversing, singing, and dancing. I had also helped them obtain a weapon, in addition to the registered weapon that they had received for self-protection, after the occurrence of several assaults on Jews.

My heart predicted evil. I made my way through the crowd and went into the offices. The entrance room was full of militia and a number of Jews standing to the side. I presented my ID, and to my questions, the militia officer replied that they had been sent to confiscate all the weapons in the building.

"Why?" I asked. "They have licenses to possess weapons!"

He responded aggressively, "There is a suspicion that the Jews killed Polish children!"

Here it comes again, I said to myself, my eyes widening incredulously. Just like this, without any warning: the Jews killed Polish children... I burst into irritable laughter, "Have you all gone mad?"

The man snapped at me, "Do not laugh! There are witnesses!" I felt my scalp contracting and my hair rising on end. The man was absolutely serious and believed this despicable story, who knows where it came from.

Outside the shouting grew. The "news" spread quickly through the city, and masses continued to flow into the small street. I turned to the Jews and promised them that I would return to the office and get help. I trusted my strength and my influence... I was naive. I hurried to the office of my commander and stood dumbfounded when he answered me, "Let it go, that is not our concern. The militia will deal with it."

"But those are my friends, I want to help them!" I cried, nearly desperate.

"Yes, I know. Even so, do not get involved. It is not our department. Best not to stir up trouble..."

"Trouble, you call the lives of people who are in danger!" I said in my heart. I could not make a sound, as I suddenly realized that my new life was an illusion.

I went down to the Security Services garage, took a jeep with a driver, and ordered him to drive to Pallanti Street. Maybe the situation had changed? No. The mayhem in the street had increased, policemen standing left and right, mostly keeping watch over those young men and women who had tried to escape from the building. Afterward, I found out that the city police commander, Gabizdowicz, a known anti-Semite, had been alerted, and he had responded that he had nobody to send, they were all on days off. The security branch of the army sent a car with soldiers, who broke into the building using their bayonets. Realizing the seriousness of the matter, I decided that I had to change my course of action immediately.

I shook off my feeling of powerlessness. We quickly returned to the office, parked the Jeep, and I instructed the driver to prepare a covered truck. I ran to my room, put on my uniform, with my gun strapped to my waist and an automatic rifle in my hand. I avoided my coworkers, ran downstairs, and called to the driver to return to the street of the mayhem. I knew that time was against me and that I was going against my superior's orders, but the driver did not know that and he followed my instructions as usual. With trepidation and difficulty, we approached.

My plan had been to approach the building with the truck and to load the people inside onto it, but we got as far as about twenty meters from the entrance and it was impossible to press forward without running over the gathered crowds. With the help of soldiers, I crossed through the crowd, with my rifle in hand. The weapon was threatening, pointing at the shouting people and directing them to the sides.

I told the policemen what I had in mind and the Jews decided to try to get out under the cover of the police and the soldiers. These created two lines with a narrow space between them, through which the besieged young people could pass. The kibbutz members descended one by one.

"Walk fast, but with confidence. Do not show them that you are afraid," I said. I went down first and stood on the back of the truck. With one hand, I pulled the climber up, still holding the rifle in the other, aiming it at the crowd. There was shouting all around: "Death to murderers! Death to the Jews!"

The escapees passed through the narrow passage and the atmosphere heated up. Suddenly someone exited the building holding a large bag. The crowd went crazy, smelling prey and loot. One of the soldiers standing in the line stuck his foot out, and the Jew stumbled and fell, his bag tumbling with him. The soldier bent over, opened the bag, and threw it towards the crowd who rose up like an enormous wave. The masses stormed the flying papers and bank notes among them.

The screams sounded like the roar of a stampede, monsters. Humanity was once more revealed in all its ugliness. The passage closed. It was nearly impossible to tell who was a soldier and who a citizen. I cocked my gun and fired into the air. The exploding sound was swallowed up by the din of the shouting, and nobody noticed. One of the survivors on the truck burst into tears and covered his face with both hands.

We waited, but nobody else came out of the house. To our horror, we suddenly saw two young people thrown off the roof, their bodies smashing on the pavement. The truck began to sway from side to side. The maddened mob was attempting, roaring with laughter, to push the truck over onto its side. The driver started the engine and drove, gripped with fear, into the crowd. People were pushed aside, crushed by the wheels and screaming in panic. I looked at the automatic rifle in my hand, with its power to destroy dozens of people, and I cursed myself and the mob and my commander and all of life. I could not pull the trigger. I could not shoot those wild human animals. I myself wanted to shout, to cry, to go mad, but the expression on my face remained frozen.

The truck pulled out and headed toward the office. Just before entering the yard, I stopped the driver, helped out the few that had been saved, who hurried away to safety. I returned to my room. For some time I sat and stared at the wall. The world that I lived in and in which I intended to go on living—was ruined. Again, I owe them nothing. I knew that I could expect punishment for my actions. I remembered the "kibbutz" members' stories about the land of Israel.

I went out to the reception room and was met with another tumultuous scene. I listened to what was being said, until the picture emerged: a crying, worked up woman had come to the police with a wild, wailing boy. She said that her son had been playing in Pallanti Street. Someone had come and given him a package, telling him to deliver the package to house number 7. As he entered the house, Jews caught him by the arms, beat him hard, and put him in the basement. There he saw, according to him, the corpses of dead children. He screamed and beat the walls, but nobody answered. After several attempts, he managed to break a board on one of the windows and escape to his home. When he arrived and told his story, a commotion arose. People began shouting and she rushed to call the police. Her son was dragged after her. He was frightened by the chaos all around him and burst into tears several times. The police interrogated him and he repeated his story again and again.

The people telling these "facts" were angry. They looked at me with hostility. I returned to my room.

The pogrom lasted for several days. A curfew was declared, and four days of terror and frenzy settled over the city and even nearby towns. There were incidents of abuse of Jewish passengers on the trains; people were beaten and robbed in the streets; many injured were brought to the hospital. The bodies of the dead were sent to the municipal morgue on wooden carts, and people threw stones at it as it passed through the streets... There was a feeling that these riots were not spontaneous; there was some hand directing them.

In the militia's search of the Jewish community building, they did not find any corpses of dead children, obviously. In the base-

ment, where the boy had broken the board over the window—
there were no windows at all. It was closed and contained only
some furniture in need of repair and everything was covered
with dust. Nobody had reported the disappearance or absence
of any Polish child. The only dead children to be found in the
city were Jewish children, killed by the rioters... In the community building they found thirteen defiled corpses of Jews. To my
knowledge, forty-eight Jews were killed in the riots.

When the militia half-heartedly reported that they had not
found anything, the investigation was transferred to the local
security services. On the third day of the riots, the building
was upset by the arrival of a most distinguished guest, General
Ratkevitz, the minister responsible for the Security Services, who
joined the investigators.

When they put real pressure on the child, on account of whom
the riots had begun, he burst into tears and admitted that his
mother "and another man" had forced him to tell the story. His
mother had repeated the story to him over and over until he
knew it by heart, and the man even hit him and tore his clothes.
The mother also fell apart before the experienced interrogators.
She admitted that the whole affair had been staged by a bakery
owner who had offered her a large sum of money. He had even
threatened her that her child would be killed if she did not cooperate. This man was also caught, and in his interrogation it
was found that this was an underground operation, intended to
topple the new regime. Underground members were scattered
throughout the city and immediately began rioting after hearing
the boy's story. The baker claimed that he had received orders
from London. The timing of the riots was determined by the
presence of many foreign journalists in the city, and indeed the
matter was making waves all over the world.

I was very excited, as a Jew, by the visit of Yitzhak Zukerman, "Antek," from the former Warsaw ghetto. He was a representative of the Center for the Unification of Polish Jews and had come to Kielce to check what had happened. I did not have a direct connection with him, except for the report that I had sent him. I was proud of the special treatment and respect that were granted him. I suppose that it was thanks to his involvement that the government organized a special train to save the victims of Kielce and transport them to Lodz.

General Ratkevitz, the Security Services commissioner, ordered the banning of the head of the militia and the local commander of the security services for not preventing the disturbance. Several militia members were punished for their participation in the pogrom. But to me it all just looked like an effort to prove the regime's innocence and no real desire to explain the actual facts of the terrible event to the people.

While our commander was in prison, the usual activities in the building continued, and nobody reported my actions. I continued to go about dressed in uniform and figure out what to do. I could not have imagined that I was going to have another grave experience that would remake my life once again.

XVIII.

The "Escape" to Czechoslovakia

The riots across the city quieted down. The occasional quarrel would break out here and there but with police pressure, it diminished. On the morning of the fourth day of the pogrom, we were notified that one of our men had been hurt, was lying wounded in his home and we would have to bring him a doctor and an investigator. I was sent to accompany the doctor, and as it was not far, we walked there. Close to the house of the wounded man, we ran into three young men, wild and filthy, that fell upon us with rude cries and it was clear that they had participated in the riots. I was dressed in uniform and wearing a weapon, which increased their anger. The three men waved their arms in our faces and one of them mimicked the doctor. "I am a doctor. I am going to visit a patient!" The doctor cried. The three rioters did not listen.

"Do you treat Jews? You love Jews, don't you? Maybe you are a Jew?" They mocked with malicious laughter. Evil grins rose to their lips. They reached for the doctor and his bag. I ordered them to leave him alone, but one of them tried to grab my weapon from me. Instantly I turned, pulled the trigger, not letting go, and the three slumped on the road, their bodies bent in different positions. We got out of there and ran to the patient's house in a state of shock. Only after we recovered from the incident did the doctor treat the patient and order that he be taken to the hospital.

The doctor said that I could not report the incident. "No one will believe that they started it," he said indignantly. "They will accuse you of murdering them out of revenge. It would be better that you keep quiet and that they don't know who did it." I knew well that even if I did not report it, I no longer had a place with the Security Services. I had to get out of there immediately, but first I would have to take the things I would need.

We returned to the office. In the street there was already a loud crowd gathered and a police horn was heard. I entered my office and locked the door. I hid my little gun in my boot and covered it with a sock. I tucked another, larger gun, of the "P38" variety, into my holster. At the last moment, I pushed two grenades into my belt and looked regretfully at the remaining ammunition in the closet that I would not be able to take with me for lack of space. I filled my pockets with different papers, several stamps and certificates, and went to the inner, hidden drawer to take my money. I hid the packet of money in the inside pocket of my jacket and draped the broad officer's cape over everything. I was overloaded and wondered how I would manage laden as I was. I could not take a rucksack since it would attract suspicion. I took the automatic rifle and glanced at the clock: at six, the special train was to leave for Lodz and I would be on it.

I went to my apartment, next to the office building, and gathered my few souvenirs: a number of photographs of myself, papers, and certificates that I had acquired since my release from the camp and a few valuables.

I hurried to the house of friends where were about fifty Jews had gathered during the pogrom. There I stirred up much excitement, telling them that I would join those leaving to Lodz.

There were those who argued that to leave now was particularly dangerous, and we would surely be harassed on the way. I did not tell them what had happened that same day, as I did not want to worry them. They tried to convince me that it was a shame to leave my job and my position in which I could help others. Others argued that we just had to wait until it was all over and then we could all return to our lives.

I stood by and felt that I had already experienced something similar to this. My family, relatives, and neighbors had responded just the same way when I had tried to convince them to escape from Ostroweic... In the end, twenty of them decided to join me, including a youth named Hainek, who I had met just recently, and with whom I had quite interesting conversations. I respected his intelligence and was happy for the friendship.

The train was already full of passengers, many of whom were injured and wounded. Evidently, the hospital had transferred those wounded in the riots to be treated in Lodz, and many were accompanied by family members. My friends dispersed throughout the different train cars. Hainek tried to convince me not to go to Lodz but to go with him to Austria. We stood on the steps of the train car and argued, and suddenly I saw someone signaling to me and running towards the train car.

"Mjetek, they are calling you to the office!" It was one of the clerks from our office. The train sounded a warning siren.

"How come?" I shouted to him, "They sent me to accompany the train!"

"No! They called that off. They need you for something else!" he shouted to me.

I gripped the door handle. "I can't come back just now, but I will be back tomorrow!" The man got closer and pulled hard at my cape.

"You aren't going anywhere! You killed Poles and now you are escaping! Come immediately to investigation!"

The cat was out of the bag... I drew my gun from its holster. "Get out of here!" I ordered sharply, "So nothing bad should befall you too!"

Hainek, who was avidly watching this event unfold, pushed me deeper into the train car and squeezed in after me. He was afraid to stay, having been seen talking to me. The train set off, gaining speed as the man was still waving his arms and calling after us. The plan had been to travel directly to Lodz, without stopping, in order to avoid harassment along the way. I told the curious Hainek briefly of what had happened that day, so that he would not pester me about it. Now I was considered a public enemy. It was possible that the police might already be waiting for me at the train station in Lodz, having gotten a message to arrest me. I implored Hainek to distance himself from me, to avoid getting mixed up in my troubles.

"I am not worried. You will look after me!" He said, smiling. We began to conceive other plans, and as the train entered the city, slowing down, we jumped from it, ran to the station and boarded a tram into the city. Hainek took me to the house of people he knew, where we spent the night.

We knew that we had to get out of Poland at any cost. We considered all of the possible options. Hainek's friends had gotten us maps of the region, dated though they were. Finally we decided to head towards Czechoslovakia. We would have to reach the town of Reichenbach, close to the Czech border, and find a way to cross the border. In Czechoslovakia, we would find a way to continue on. I filled out the appropriate forms for myself, according to which I was going, as part of my job, with my clerk, to an investigation in Reichenbach. We bade our hosts a warm goodbye and set off.

In Reichenbach, we went to find Jews. We were sent to a branch of the "Zionist Worker" that had established a "kibbutz" for preparation. We were received by the secretary, who was somewhat startled by me in my uniform. We asked for help crossing the border. "For that you will need eight thousand zlotys, four thousand each," the secretary informed us.

We did not have that kind of money. "But I have something worth more than money!" I showed him my automatic rifle and told him that I also had a pistol and grenades in my possession. His eyes lit up at the sight of the weapon. "Look," he said excitedly, "Go to a hotel and rest. I will contact the person you need and work out the details. Come back in two days. But don't run away from us!" He added with a smile, shaking our hands goodbye.

We spent two days at the hotel. We barely walked about the streets but rather passed the time telling stories and making plans. The land of Israel featured prominently in our conversations. We exchanged all the minimal information that we had about Israel and tried to learn several words in Hebrew. The Hebrew language sounded very difficult, and Hainek said, "There is no need to worry. There will be Jews there from Poland, we can speak with them in Polish or Yiddish..."

At the "Zionist Worker" office, it seemed that our assets were more desirable than money. They even wanted my uniform and supplied me, in exchange, with simple civilian clothes, which they tailored to fit me.

The next day, early in the morning, we were already in Czechoslovakia. Our group numbered nine people. We traveled part of the way on a closed truck, until we reached the forest. There we met our guide. We went on foot, walking quickly, and when our guide stopped us before descending a small hill, we were very tired and sweaty. My new clothes made walking hard for me and constrained my steps. The guide pointed to the hill across from us. "See that group of trees there, in that direction? That is a Czech transit station. Walk straight there. They will let you through without any trouble. They are alright!"

They really were alright. We were greeted with a few questions, they asked us for cigarettes, and showed us to a small office, in which we received hot, sweet tea and slices of bread spread with jam. Some time later, an old, ugly van showed up and shuttled us to the city Bratislava, our first stop in Czechoslovakia. We were taken to a hotel named "Yellen" and we found ourselves among Jews.

The hotel was rented out by agents and served as a transit camp for the escape organizations, managed by delegates from Palestine and local Jews. We had joined up with thousands of Jews, refugees, waiting for their turn to go to Israel. The hotel was well-organized. In addition to the crowded lodgings, there were rooms for different activities: learning Hebrew, history, lifestyle in Israel and then, a sort of mini-training for the new lives that awaited us.

In the courtyard were held general conferences, with the speaker standing on a balcony addressing all of us together. After greetings and some introductory statements, they would announce lists of those leaving and instructions.

At the first gathering in which we participated, all newcomers were told, after the welcome, that we had to submit all of our papers at the head office, including documents and photographs, that might help to identify us or hint at the places we had run away from.

"Everything will be returned to you when we arrive in Israel," the man promised, "Nothing will be lost. Try to learn Hebrew as quickly as possible, so that we can deceive the British if they catch us when we get there. From today forth, if someone asks you where you are from, say that you are from Greece. None of them know Greek anyway."

After the speech was finished, the gathering dispersed and we went to the office to hand over our papers. My turn came. I gave them my packet of papers, wrapped and bound. The clerk looked up at me, "Did you hand over everything?"

"I kept three photographs," I answered. "They are not compromising."

To my surprise, the man leaped from his seat in anger. "Do you not understand what we told you? Who are you to decide which photographs are dangerous? They told you to give us everything, so hand it over!"

I was dumbfounded. "This is how you talk to me? I have to get this kind of treatment from you too?" I said, as angry as he was.

"It does not please you? You can stay here!" He shoved my shoulder.

"Even here? From a Jew! Listen!" I said to him, taking control of myself with great difficulty, "I also know how to speak crudely, and I also learned how to give orders. Do not yell at me! I still do not owe you anything!"

The man reddened with anger, "So? What will you do to me? Who are you? If you do not do what you are told, you will never get out of here!"

The people standing behind me began to speak all at once in protest. The man got closer, as though preparing to push me outside. I bent down and pulled my small pistol from my boot. I felt close to losing control, but again I felt overcome by the feeling that I no longer cared about anything. I pointed the gun at him.

"I ran away from them. I am not running away from you! If

you are unable to behave decently to people—go back to where you came from! Do not raise your hands to people! Sit in your seat," I said and pointed with my gun towards his chair, "and do the job that they put you here to do!"

The man, stunned, lost his voice and sat in his place. The room fell silent. I returned my gun to its place and went back to my room. Hainek followed after me, "Don't get so worked up, Mjetek. Not everyone is like him. He is tired and irritable. Don't take it to heart!"

I was quiet. I did not leave the room and nobody disturbed me until the morning. The following day, during the assembly, they informed us that we would be leaving on a train to Austria and would be going to Vienna. "The tickets are ready. It is forbidden, under all circumstances, to speak Yiddish, Polish, or Czech. We are registered as Greeks returning to their homeland, to Greece!" The assembly was dismissed.

On my way back to my room I was stopped by an Israeli man and his translator. "Are you the owner of the gun?" He asked me directly in Hebrew, his voice quiet, sure of himself. He observed me curiously while the translator conveyed what he had said in a monotonous voice. "I want to apologize for my man. He was reprimanded, and we hope that there will be no recurrence." He waited for the translator to finish.

I did not answer. "I saw your papers," he continued. "Maybe you would like to join our organization?"

I was quiet a moment. I liked this guy, with his direct speech and warm eyes.

"I accept the apology. But I want to get to Palestine."

"You know that you cannot travel with the weapon—there may be a check and that would screw up the entire operation."

He did not order me to hand over my gun. He appealed to

my reason and judgment. I smiled at him, "Alright, you win. I will give you the gun. When we get on the train I will give it to you personally." He extended his hand. We exchanged a strong handshake, which did not require any translation. Still holding my hand, he added, "If you change your mind regarding joining our organization, you can do so along the way too, at the next stations!" He smiled and went on his way. My peace of mind returned and I joined the Hebrew class.

XIX.

Vienna - Marseilles - Haifa - Cyprus

We set off to Vienna on a rickety, primitive train. I had made a cover for my little gun, which disguised its shape, and I parted from it, handing it over to that Israeli man through the train window. I added, "I wish you great success!"

He waved his hand slightly in a movement similar to a salute and smiled. His image stayed with me long after he had disappeared from my sight. If there are many like him it will all be ok, I thought hopefully.

In Vienna, we stayed in hospital building named for Rothschild, from which Jews had been sent in every direction on their various escape routes, whose ultimate goal was the land of Israel. The conditions were similar to those of the previous transit camp. The suggestion of my anonymous friend, to join the escape organization, stuck in my mind, and when I was called to speak with the leaders, who repeated the offer—I found myself answering in the affirmative.

A process of registration, training, and new certifications began. My documents were returned to me and I signed a form which put me on the payroll of the Joint (The American Jewish Joint Distribution Committee). At the end of the acclimatization phase, I was sent to the transit camp in Kleinmagen, in order to arrange a security police force there.

Once more, I parted ways with Hainek and other friends. The arrangements were made quickly and I had no time to regret my sudden decision. I had not given up on immigrating to Israel but rather postponed my arrival. What's the rush? Here, too, I could do important work for my homeland.

In the Kleinmagen camp were put under my command, a group of young men from "kibbutzim" in Poland, Hungary, and Romania, and even a few Jews from Russia. Our role was to maintain order at the camp, to prevent fights or theft, to oversee the admissions and exits of refugees. I quickly adjusted to the role and the place. I got to know some Israelis and I loved their courage, their joie de vivre, and their naivety. I learned many Hebrew words and settled into a routine.

As the days became weeks, which became months, the routine became oppressive. Anyone could do my job, I thought to myself. What will become of me? What is the purpose of anything? Am I waiting for something, for some sort of change to occur? There would not be any change here.

I talked a lot with the guys, and one evening, during conversation, someone came up with an intriguing idea: he said that in the nearby city of Linz, there had been ads published by the French government looking for volunteers for their Foreign Legion. "Whoever serves the Legion for three years," the notices said, "will be granted French citizenship." All of us lacked citizenship and the idea of obtaining citizenship of so stable and safe a place as France fascinated us. The idea began to take shape, and after an impassioned argument, two of the guys got up and declared that they would do it no matter what. I was also taken by the idea and announced that I would join them.

The next day, we requested the day off, which was approved

without difficulty, as it was Saturday. We went to the recruitment office in Linz. The large hall was busy and bustling, as the volunteers' transport was preparing to leave for Morocco on Sunday morning. We hurried to the information office, where we were directed to the registration rooms. We were told that we could register with any name we liked and there was no need for certificates. The one condition: medical examinations. If we passed them, we would have to sign a commitment to serve for three years in any task that might be required. We were soon brought before the doctors, who began to perform an intensive round of check-ups. The doctor observed my scars with curiosity but did not say a thing, until he got to my teeth. Evidently, I was missing three teeth and as such was unfit to serve in the French Foreign Legion...

"If you were only missing two, that would be fine." The doctor said, "But three is over the maximum. Sorry!" Seeing the disappointment on my face he added, "You know what? Go into town and find a dentist to make you a false tooth. Then I can let you pass the test!" I grabbed my clothes, dressed quickly, and ran to the city. In the entire city of Linz, I could not find a dentist who would agree to make me a fake tooth that same day.

The volunteer transport went to Morocco without me. I returned to Kleinmagen with mixed feelings, without my friends, who had been deemed fit for service. The whole episode had been so fleeting and so hasty, that I did not know whether or not to regret it. One of the first things I did upon my return was to approach the camp dentist and request dental treatment...

Over the next months, I received two letters from my enlisted friends, describing their many adventures and wanderings. The third letter came in an official envelope from the French government, to inform me—the only person whose address the soldiers had had with them—that they had been killed while carrying out their military duties in the training camp in Algiers. Depressed by the news of my friends' death, I tried to find out details of the disaster, but the answer that I received much later was that they would not disclose secret information, and they attached to this a description of the place of their burial and what had been written on their gravestones.

While I was still pondering the fate of my friends, amazed at the vicissitudes of fate, I received another letter. One morning, as the mail was being handed out, I heard someone call to me, "Mjetek, there's a letter for you!"

A letter for me? I raced over to the office. I gripped the letter with shaking hands and burst out in excitement: Isser! Isser Gerber from Ostrowiec, who had escaped from the factory we were in before Auschwitz! Isser, my friend who had saved me when I was terribly wounded by the fire! Isser, who I had assumed was dead... He wrote briefly that he was in Germany, heard that I was staying at the camp from someone who had been here. He pleaded that I come to him, and attached his address...

At that same time I was supposed to lead a group of escapees to Belgium. I informed the management that I had to leave. I was forced to go. I had discovered someone alive... The only one who remained from my previous world. I was firm in my decision and my mission was transferred to someone else. I said goodbye once more and went to Munich. In January 1947, I met Isser in an emotional reunion.

We lived together for two months. We ate at the community kitchen or cooked for ourselves, walking around from place to place and talking. We spoke and we remembered and we told stories. And again I was gripped by a kind of restlessness. I could not tolerate the Germans. I wanted to leave. I was pursued by thoughts of Israel. Isser decided to join me, and having contacted all of our possible connections, we finally gained the status of illegal immigrants.

We were sent to a village "kibbutz" of Jews who were soon to migrate to Israel. The kibbutz had once been a large German farm, and there were about eighty Jews there. To my amazement, there were some among them who remembered the story of my intervention, trying to rescue the group of Jews in the city of Kielce, and they welcomed us with open arms. From this small village, near Munich, we were transferred by trucks to another camp. This was in the city of Dachau, not far from the terrible concentration camp, in a residential area that used to house the SS soldiers and had been designated by the German government to serve as a reception and transition area for refugees. There were already around four hundred people waiting there. In a convoy of trucks, accompanied by Israeli "defense" personnel, we headed for France. At the Strasbourg border station, the convoy split, with each group of trucks headed in a different direction. They did not tell us where we were going or how they had reached an agreement with the French police. We continued on our way until the small town of Plisan, next to the port city of Marseilles. "We are in France!" My friends in the truck rejoiced.

We found ourselves once again in a small transit camp. There were already Jews there who had come from Belgium, religious people of the "Mizrachi" movement. Isser and I roamed the camp and even went out to visit the town and get to know the area. We exchanged our money for French currency and bought clothes and food. We even attended a folk dance that took place in town and were welcomed by the local residents.

We left the Plisan camp on the eve of Passover, in March 1947. We got to the Marseilles port and boarded the ship, "Theodor Herzl." The flag of Panama was flying from the mast, the captain was Mordechai (Moka) Limon, and we were Jews sailing to the land of Israel.

We walked aboard the ship with great excitement and hope. Several prayed. We were instructed gently but forcefully to go down into the belly of the ship, and to stay there. The number of passengers boarding must not be seen, though if someone had heard, they would hardly have believed it. At the time of sailing, the ship bore nearly three thousand passengers... Much work had gone into preparations to handle this huge number, and the main calculation had been to take as many people as possible—without consideration for comfort. The hold of the ship had been completely cleared of partitions, walls, or unnecessary objects. In the large hall, rows of bunks had been built—many many narrow bunks, five levels high, and half a meter between rows. There were thousands of lying spaces for thousands of people, refugees who did not sleep well under favorable conditions, from whom sighs and screams would erupt even while they were asleep. Men, women, and children in conditions that reminded us of *that* crowding and *those* bunks... But what an enormous difference! We were one big family, finally going home. Family, that despite all the differences of opinion, and the desire to find a comfortable place, to do well, despite everything, knew how to break into song every so often. Only a few complained of the difficulties, but many quieted them, saying, "So what? We all want to get home! Just a little more difficulty and we will get there..."

The food was meager: canned food and crackers. The water was scarce: two bottles per person per day. We knew thirst and we knew filth and we knew bad smells. There were even attempts to steal water. Human weaknesses were revealed. But most of the passengers suffered quietly, understanding. We knew that it would end and there was a reason to suffer this discomfort, that it was worthwhile.

We were only permitted to go up to the deck at night to get fresh air, to cleanse our lungs from the crowded space. During the days, we lay on our bunks, conversed, and learned Hebrew from one another. People sang songs and recited all that they knew, and the din was loud. During the nights, we would sit on the deck in families and groups, and make plans.

We tried not to think of the bitter possibility that we could be stopped by the British. From time to time, there were evacuations: at the sound of a siren, we had to quickly disappear from the deck, so as not to be seen by the passengers on passing ships or pilots of planes flying over the sea.

We knew that our chance of breaking through the blockade ring imposed by the British on the shores of Israel was small. Those who did not know this before we set off, learned it soon after when the captain explained it to us. He would deliver speeches from atop the bridge of the deck and explained the facts skillfully and comprehensively. His confident voice and unique personality granted us a feeling of security, perhaps stronger than his own. In his confident, energetic voice, he even informed us one morning that we had been spotted by a reconnaissance plane and would probably be stopped by a destroyer.

"The women and children will remain below," he ordered. "And only the men will go up when the signal is given. We must carry out what we have decided—demonstrating against the restrictions on immigration to Palestine!" At the end, he added, "Don't worry. It will all end well!"

Four destroyers armed with cannons were sent by the British to stop the ship of survivor refugees from safely reaching the shore. We saw the beaches of Tel Aviv on the horizon and we knew that even if we were to get there, we would not stay long.

And indeed the struggle was brief.

There was a huge sign, with the words "Theodor Herzl Defense Ship" on it, spread across the side of the ship, for the eyes of hundreds of British sailors watching silently from the decks of their ships. The Israeli flag waved in place of the Panamanian one. We began to sing "Hatikvah" and we did not stop even when loudspeakers began calling out instructions to us.

Then things happened quickly: the destroyer ground against the side of the ship, ropes with hooks caught on, and armed soldiers climbed aboard, invading the deck. Our men sprayed water at the soldiers, shouted slogans, and hit back with arms, sticks, and bottles. Then bombs of tear gas were thrown at us, several of which were even shot into the belly of the ship where the women and children were. In the heat of the fight, shots were heard. There were many casualties. Shouts were coming from every direction.

The "battle" was over. The British army had beaten the Jewish enemy... But we did not see the gleam of victory in the soldiers' eyes. They evacuated the wounded and in the eyes of some, we could see shame and even pity. Those who were able refused their help. The ship was dragged to the Haifa port. We had arrived in the land of Israel... to a well-fenced English detention camp. We were sprayed with disinfectant, our belongings were scattered, and some were lost.

From the other end of the camp, we were later transferred to a closed English ship, a prison ship that took us to Cyprus. Many Greeks watched the operation of our disembarkation from the ship at the Famagusta port and accompanied the efforts of the British soldiers with cries of derision and laughter. To us they called out encouragement and blessings. On our way to the refugee camp, they threw us oranges and sweets, right into the British trucks. We took much warmth and encouragement from those friendly people.

XX.

Aboard the "Theodor Herzl" to Israel - Again

We were in a closed camp once again. Fences, sentries, shifts, disinfectant, and living in tents, crowded. Isser and I were in camp number 68, in a tent with eight others. Again, there was a new daily schedule, but it was significantly different. The camp was well organized from within by the Israeli Hagana organization. People were registered and sorted into groups. There was a rich camp life: schools, clubs, sporting activities, and secret operations—army training.

A short while after our arrival, I went to seek out the superiors. With their help, I found myself a place and a role. I was trained to be the head of one of the sports clubs on behalf of the Joint, for a salary of 15 shillings a month. My official position was to coach various sports and to develop the physical fitness of the men and women who so desired. My additional role, which nobody said explicitly, was to join the instructors who trained in the use of weapons, explosives and other tools of destruction, special training, and various wrestling maneuvers.

Order and discipline within the organization were exemplary: keeping propriety, keeping secrecy, passwords of warning and identification, plans for escaping from the camp (which succeeded a number of times), and so on. The work was endless and hard. People who had never held a weapon needed to be made into trained soldiers. They insisted on learning, and we insisted on teaching and we were able to achieve a great deal.

From time to time, "transports" were released—groups from the Youth Aliyah, sick people, or camp veterans. There were many incidents of nervous breakdowns. For some reason, there were instances of fighting between the refugees on the ship "Moledet," and the name of the ship became a kind of code word among us for 'crazy'. One of us, a man who went by the nickname Moishe, decided one day to disguise himself as "Moledet"—expressed in a smile—so that the British would send him to Israel. He had already failed in several attempts to escape, and this time he was determined to succeed. He questioned the Jewish doctors and learned the common signs of insanity. Little by little he began to demonstrate signs of mental infirmity, by all accounts, until he had practically convinced even those of us who knew his secret. Eventually, his madness progressed until it actually became dangerous—he went wild and fell upon the British soldiers. Finally, he was sent in for examinations and observation by the English doctor. He called additional doctors in for consultation. One of the doctors ruled: "This one is really crazy. He must be sent to Palestine!" Moishe did not fall into this trap but began shrieking, as he spat out, "Don't want Palestine! No!"

The doctors were convinced of Moishe's mental infirmity and he was tied up and put on the next transport to the country that he yearned for. The Israeli doctor who had been present during the examinations laughed heartily as he described the scene to us and told how Moishe had winked mischievously at him when he heard the final diagnosis.

From time to time we prepared for the arrival of more refugees. The camp was bustling in preparation for two huge ships coming from Romania—"Pan York" and "Pan Crescent"—each of which bore many thousands of illegal immigrants. Some of them were coming from our previous camp.

A group of young men from the "Zionist Youth" was housed in a row of tents opposite us. A rumor emerged that they had cigarettes and were selling them for cheap. I entered the tent, divided by a cloth partition, in which three young women and two men were residing. I bought cigarettes and returned and bought more cigarettes and looked at the nice girls with growing interest. One day I summoned up my courage and invited the liveliest of the girls to a dance at the clubhouse. She agreed, but on one condition: her friend would join us, as she was "shy like that, not the going out type."

We got to the clubhouse, where there were dances on Friday evenings and holidays. The place was full, and we looked for a corner to sit. While we were walking around, a young, energetic acquaintance of mine joined our group and asked permission to dance with my partner. I was left with the other, the quiet one. I found her a place to sit and observed her. For some reason I felt no need to talk. After some time, I held my hand out to her and pulled her after me to dance. We danced, and our steps and rhythm were marvelously well matched. We continued to dance and out of the corner of my eye, I saw my friend looking for me to return my partner to me. With a gesture, I hinted to him to keep her busy and I did not let go of my quiet partner. "Sara," she told me with a shy laugh. It was late in the evening when I accompanied her back to the tent, choosing a long, roundabout route, and while we walked, we spoke.

From that evening on, we met often and spent our evenings with her friends. One of them, named Miki, turned to us one day and casually requested that we come serve as witnesses—he and his girlfriend were going to register for marriage. We showed up to the office at the appointed time and signed the forms, indicating that we knew them and that they were unattached and so on, and we prepared to leave. Suddenly Miki spun around and said to the Rabbi managing the registration, "Now register this couple. They also want to get married."

We looked at one another for what felt like a long time. Sara said nothing, just her eyes sparkled. Without a word, we turned to the Rabbi, who had already pulled out an additional form. Our names were written. "Date?" Asked the Rabbi. "Same as them," I replied.

I held Sara's hand tightly. The date was written. The witnesses signed. We left, hand in hand, excited and stunned.

One week later, we had the ceremony, followed by the double wedding party. The party was modest, and the refreshments consisted mainly of oranges, but the enthusiasm and joy of all the guests who participated was very great. The only shadow on our happiness was the memory of those who were not there.

As a wedding gift from the Hagana headquarters, I received a very special present: a private cell to live in, constructed from tin. The hut was one of the luxuries of the officials in the camp, and divided into four cells by a tin partition...

Then Sara's turn came to immigrate to Israel. Despite her protests, I managed to convince her to go, and not to give up her chance. "I will come after you, soon," I comforted her when we parted. "You will start our home there!"

We were still in exile in Cyprus, when the speakers declared in a shaky and emotional voice that the State of Israel had been established. About fifteen thousand people broke into singing and excited dancing. We sat around huge bonfires and expressed our concerns about the fate of the young state.

Rumors and news of the war raging in Israel clouded our efforts to end the organization of the release of tens of thousands of people. The "Hagana" members were the last to leave Cyprus.

On an Israeli ship, bearing the flag of Israel, and named—amazingly, as though things had been directed from above—"Theodor Herzl," I arrived, in the month of January 1949, to the land of Israel. Already on board, we had received orders for enlistment and instructions to register and organize in the new army, the Israel Defense Forces.

We looked hungrily out over the truck at the Israeli landscape. We got to the army camp at Beit Lid. The country was at war and I had not yet seen my wife and I did not know anything about how she was doing. I only knew that she was in a small settlement in the south of Israel called Gedera, together with her friend. This I told to the soldier dressed in strange clothes, which was either military uniform or a costume, who wrote down my name and other details. There was a brief consultation and I was called in to talk.

"We wanted to send you to an accelerated officers' course," said one of the commanders. "But in the meantime there has been a change. You know where Gedera is?"

"No," I replied, "But I know that it is in the South." "That's right," said the man. "And the war is not far from there. The situation is not good. If you want to join your wife, there will be plenty of work for you. Go to Gedera and get in touch with the military there."

I received directions as to how to get to Gedera. When I arrived, I held Sara tight in my arms for hours. I settled in and filled my roles as lookout and security, until the threat of the Egyptian army got farther away, and we took on other positions.

In Gedera, we set up our house, where we raised our two

children: Zehava—named for my mother, and Yehezkel, named for my brother.

As an epilogue, I will add a few things.

Over the years, I met survivors from Ostrowiec in Israel. I heard rumors of my brother's death. I discovered my cousin Yizhak who possessed several pictures of members of my family, which he had managed to save from before. Just the two of us remained, from the entire family.

Let it be in my story that this is a tribute to the memory of those who were lost...

Mjetek in the Security Services

ReadMore Press

DISCOVERING THE NEXT BESTSELLER

Would you like a
FREE WWII historical
fiction audiobook?

This audiobook is valued at 14.99$ on Amazon and is exclusively free for Readmore Press' readers!

To get your free audiobook, and to sign up for our newsletter where we send you more exclusive bonus content every month,

Scan the QR code

Readmore Press is a publisher that focuses on high-end, quality historical fiction. We love giving the world moving stories, emotional accounts, and tear-filled happy endings.

We hope to see you again in our next book!

Never stop reading, Readmore Press